T0293052

"*The Essence of Leadership* reminds one to reflect on self, emphasizing the importance of individual growth and adaptability in driving meaningful change and leading others effectively. A unique personal development resource, it is a complex read that helps navigate one's lived experiences, to understand better how we manage our values, styles, and emotions in the context of leading others towards common goals."

Barbara Walczyk Joers
President and CEO
Gillette Children's Specialty Healthcare
Minnesota, USA

"As one who strives to be the best leader I can, I have read many books on the subject. What Anderson and Hamman have done here is refreshing and engaging, framing leadership beyond the usual sets of skills found in many 'how to' books on the subject. The authors provide a keen perspective rooted in family systems theory, creating an impactful resource I will revisit on my path to continuously improving my performance as a leader."

David M. Aronoff, MD, FIDSA, FAAM
John B. Hickam Professor of Medicine
Chair, Department of Medicine
Indiana University School of Medicine
545 Barnhill Dr., EH 305
Indianapolis, IN 46202

"Leadership is largely about emotions, and managing one's own emotions, and others'; the emotions operating in an organization is a critical skill. Understanding common emotions such as anxiety and how it operates at these three levels is crucial if you want to be someone others are willing to follow, for managing processes of change, and for the complex work of growing and developing healthier leaders, teams, and organizations. Anderson and Hamman have provided an indispensable resource for just these goals. It is a text I will assign in my leadership classes."

Barbara J. McClure, MDiv., PhD
Associate Professor: Pastoral Theology and Practice
Director: Flourishing in Ministry Program
Brite Divinity School at TCU
Fort Worth, TX

"Thankfully, a book about leadership, proposing that solid leadership begins in the affective, the soul, rather than the cognitive. Blending the best of family systems theory with cognitive rational dynamics, the reader understands leadership as an integration of both heart and head. A must-read for all clergy."

Donald W. Winslett, Ed.D
Director
Center for Clergy Care and Education
Pensacola, FL

"These are hard times in which to be a leader. Virtually every industry, whether nonprofit, faith community, or corporation, is experiencing massive disruption. Hamman and Anderson provide a framework for 'self-differentiated leaders' who can think, feel, and discern their way through the knotty task of leadership, finding a path that is good for the organization, those it serves, and even for leaders themselves."

Dr. Shari K. Brink
President and CEO
Blanton-Peale Institute & Counseling Center
New York, NY

"You just may meet yourself in *The Essence of Leadership*. I did. Anderson and Hamman know that we all lead from the inside out. They say the hard things out loud. And in so doing they build trust with us as readers and give us confidence, courage, and wisdom to become less anxious versions of ourselves and steadier, more resilient and effective leaders."

John Luth
Chaplain
The Salvation Army – Edmonton Centre of Hope
Alberta and Northern Territories Division

"Authors Anderson and Hamman draw on lived experience having personally engaged a wide variety of intense leadership environments and the anxiety that permeates them. Pairing deep knowledge of both psychological theory and the management space, they elevate the truth that anxiety drives both reactive leadership systems and the individual leaders who seek to make changes within them.
Their thoughts will resonate as leaders are encouraged toward the personal health of managing one's own anxieties, which then cannot help but bring a way through as well as lead the organization into greater health."

Ann Shackelton
VP Human Resources Mission Care & Enrichment
Young Life

"Derek and Jaco draw on their diverse backgrounds and leadership experiences to provide a useful guidebook to the aspiring leader in all of us. *The Essence of Leadership* reminds us that the best leaders are able to master their emotional selves before effectively leading others. As a business leader in today's fast-paced, competitive environment, I have learned that behind every high-performing team is a high-performing leader."

David H. Dupuy
CEO
Community Healthcare Trust, Inc.

"In *The Essence of Leadership*, Jaco Hamman and Derek Anderson offer a true gift: a moral vision of leadership that is abundant with psychological wisdom. They draw on the resources of family systems theory in an original way that is sure to transform both individuals and institutions. In the leadership literature, there has never been a book as emotionally rich as this one."

Nathan Carlin
Director of the McGovern Center for Humanities and Ethics
Samuel Karff Chair
McGovern Medical School

"Anderson and Hamman underscore the inescapable paradox embedded within any effort to attain a thriving organization: To lead others well, one must lead oneself first. If you want to excel as a leader, with the ability to form relationships for success, they invite you to embark on a path of deliberate and personal transformation, away from burnout and despair toward durable and sustainable efficacy for you and your organization."

Rev. Dr. Katherine Wiebe, PsyD, PhD
Organizational and Leadership Consultant
Founder, Institute for Collective Trauma and Growth

"Human interaction is a complex web of relationships and interconnectedness that requires us to see through the patterns that have been forged though our family systems. By using family systems theory, the authors help us disrupt unconstructive patterns in our interactions with others, thus putting us on a pathway to real cooperation."

Rosemarie Henkel-Rieger
Co-director
Southeast Center for Cooperative Development

The Essence of Leadership

The world is experiencing a leadership crisis. *The Essence of Leadership* addresses this concern by empowering self-differentiated leadership. The authors draw on family systems thinking, foundational to family therapy, psychodynamic theory, a recognized lens on human nature, and proven process management tools. The core message explored over seven chapters is that a leader's management of their own anxiety and the anxiety in a system has direct implications for their effectiveness in bringing change.

The authors believe that leadership is mastering emotional and relational processes seeking to bring change according to clearly defined goals and ethical principles. As such, leadership is poorly defined as a cognitive-rational, economic, charismatic, democratic, data-based, or expert-driven "How to ..." skill. Rather, anxiety's flow and management greatly determine the likelihood of systemic transformation.

After reading this book, leaders will be empowered with a growing understanding of the role anxiety plays in systemic change even as they are equipped to lead with less anxiety. Though the theory and practices in the book are applicable to all leaders, leadership is illustrated through numerous case studies from their extensive experience empowering leaders in both the for profit and nonprofit sectors. Callouts throughout the book, along with questions for reflection, invite the reader into deeper contemplation.

The Essence of Leadership

Maintaining Emotional Independence in Situations Requiring Change

Derek W. Anderson
Jaco J. Hamman

Routledge
Taylor & Francis Group

A PRODUCTIVITY PRESS BOOK

First published 2024
by Routledge
605 Third Avenue, New York, NY 10158

and by Routledge
4 Park Square, Milton Park, Abingdon, Oxon, OX14 4RN

Routledge is an imprint of the Taylor & Francis Group, an informa business

ISBN: 978-1-032-73483-5 (hbk)
ISBN: 978-1-032-73398-2 (pbk)
ISBN: 978-1-003-46399-3 (ebk)

DOI: 10.4324/9781003463993

Typeset in ITC Garamond Std
by Deanta Global Publishing Services, Chennai, India

To all who, either by choice or by circumstance, find themselves leading and decide to do well.

Contents

List of Figures

List of Tables

Preface

Leadership is affirming and a thrill. It is also challenging and taxing. We know. Our shared experience spans more than sixty years of leadership in a variety of contexts ranging from corporate, industrial, and healthcare corporations (Derek) to academic, nonprofit, and ecclesial institutions (Jaco). Of course, we've been led by others since early childhood. Reflecting on being led we have to admit most often that the leadership we experienced left us in frustration. Too often we were led by a proverbial Moses, the historic Jewish hero charged to lead his people out of slavery in Egypt to a promised land, only to circle aimlessly from one wilderness to another. Moses saw and came so close, but never entered the promised land that filled his dreams for years. We had leaders who brought no or little change, who could not keep their best employees, in whom we found little transparency around how decisions were made, and we witnessed how situations were left unaddressed with no clear path provided on how to achieve predefined goals. Sometimes we were a Moses, feeling frustrated and wondering if we are accomplishing anything.

Our love for teaching, mentoring, and leadership formation inspired this book. While sharing a meal, we discovered in our teaching on leadership and in our consultancy that we both draw from the same well: *family systems theory*. This theory, which evolved during and after World War II and is foundational to contemporary family therapy, identifies a family and other systems as an emotional unit. Individuals within the system react to the tension or emotion within the system, the latter determining the roles, functions, and positions people within the system will take. The emotion can present as apathy, fear, anxiety, conflict, or even resistance to change. Most often the members comprising a system react differently to the same event or stressor, complicating a leader's task to facilitate change or growth. *Leadership, we argue, is mastering an emotional and relational process within a system while seeking to bring change according to clearly defined goals and ethical principles.* As such, leadership is much more than being a cognitive-rational, economic, charismatic, democratic, or even an expert-driven process. Family systems theory, which informs every chapter, places a person at the center of leadership instead of promoting select "how to" principles. The latter, so common to leadership books, inevitably fail for two reasons: the principles often neglect the leader's self; and, it does not reckon with the emotional process in the system.

As authors we approach systems theory from different stances due to our different formational journeys and our diverse contexts. As a trained clinician, Jaco brings an inner- and interpersonal, as well as a coaching and therapeutic approach to leadership. Derek, in turn, with his engineering and business administration background, brings a process-minded, analytic approach to his leadership, mentoring, and consultancy. We share not only a foundation of systems thinking, but also a commitment to our self-differentiation, i.e., our ability to remain a thinking, discerning, and feeling person within systems dictating what one should think, what questions can be asked, and how one should feel.

We believe an excellent leader can reckon effectively with a system's emotional process, for before they engage the system's dynamics, the leader has done their work vis-à-vis the family and personal systems they are a part of. Discerning a system's emotional process, a self-differentiated leader sees things differently compared to leaders whose decisions are driven by charisma, questionable data, or a list of obscure principles. *The Essence of Leadership* seeks to empower leaders to lead differently as recognized agents of transformation and change.

Our unique educational and leadership paths inform us, but so too do our different cultures (the United Kingdom for Derek and South Africa for Jaco). We consequently approach leadership otherwise compared to the leaders we encounter in especially the United States. We are, for example, more direct in our communication than most leaders we meet. Between us we have fierce debates about leadership, society, politics, economics, and religion. We most often disagree. Such disagreements will doom many a relationship. Not so with ours. The synergy emanating from our shared friendship and our diverse professional competencies means we have talked through each chapter, read and corrected each other's work multiple times, and worked intentionally to write a book on leadership for a variety of contexts. We welcome you into our conversation, to agree or to disagree, always expanding our understanding and scholarship of competent, transformative leadership.

The need for excellent leadership is a global need. Nations seem in desperate need of transformative, compassionate, and ethical leadership. We firmly believe there are no "natural leaders," only leaders who have sought empowerment and education to lead more effectively. We recommend you avoid any leader who claims a natural giftedness to lead. It takes significant mentoring, formative experiences, and a theoretical foundation to become an excellent leader.

Though *The Essence of Leadership* is written in a user-friendly style and the concepts you will be introduced to are straightforward, it is not necessarily an "easy" book to read. We are confident you will resonate with what we will address in these pages. Emotional processes, however, resist intellectual understanding. Leaders lead with their whole beings, not just their minds. For many leaders, the eighteen or so inches between their heads and their hearts is a distance too large to bridge. We recommend reading the book, highlighting or noting what resonates and what elicits questions, talking with family members, mentors, colleagues, and friends about it, and then returning to those insights or questions over time to enable deeper personal integration. As with all worthwhile processes of formation, growing in leadership takes time and effort. In fact, such growth never really ends as opportunities for learning is a lifelong invitation. We know ongoing, never-ending processes of learning and integration are frustrating for those in search of a quick fix or for those seeking growth with no personal commitment or involvement. We believe that staying committed to engaging systems more effectively is worthwhile.

We wrote *The Essence of Leadership* to be a trustworthy, wise conversation partner. May the book transform you into being a less anxious leader, someone who is reliably innovative, a leader whose excellence builds team work and transforms systems.

Derek and Jaco
Nashville, Tennessee
October 2023

Acknowledgments

Partnerships bring possibility. We are grateful to many stakeholders who made this project stronger:

- Vanderbilt University's Owen Graduate School of Business
  and the Divinity School provided opportunities to teach
  on leadership and classrooms where students are eager to
  learn. We received time off and a research leave to complete this project.
- Those we love and hold dear experienced our absent-
  mindedness and preoccupation with differentiated
  leadership.
- Ulrike Guthrie, a seasoned independent editor, provided
  the needed feedback on pre-publication drafts and guided
  us toward publication.
- Business leaders Rick MacLean and John Siedlecki read an
  advanced draft and added their wisdom to the project.
- Kristine Rynne Mednansky, Senior Editor (*Business &
  Management; Healthcare Management*) at Routledge/
  Taylor & Francis Group made this a stronger project. We
  are grateful for her and her team's advocacy, experience,
  and professionalism.

Author Bios

 **Derek W. Anderson** is Vice-President, Business Improvement at Vanderbilt University Medical Center. An engineer holding a Master of Management in Healthcare degree, he has more than 30 years of national and international corporate experience in change management across business sectors. Derek has taught Healthcare Strategy and on adaptive change and the use of data within Vanderbilt University Owen Graduate School of Management program.

 **Jaco J. Hamman, PhD**, is Professor of Religion, Psychology, and Culture at Vanderbilt University Divinity School. A clinically trained academic, his research areas include psychodynamic theory, leadership formation, and the foundations of human flourishing. Jaco has published nine books and numerous book chapters and peer-reviewed articles. He co-founded *Our Place Nashville*, a nonprofit placing persons with developmental disabilities in intentional communities called Friendship Houses.

Introduction

A man announced he is dead.[1]

His family, neighbors, and all around him became concerned
and tried to convince him otherwise. They failed at every
attempt as he taunted them to "prove" he was not dead. When
they tried, he merely stated he was dead and thus they did
not exist. Soon those around the man, especially his wife, felt
he had gone mad and first called upon a psychiatrist, then
an evangelist. Both men failed to convince the man he was
not dead. When the psychiatrist suggested the man might be
psychotic, the man asked what therapy they would suggest for
a dead man, implying those who would try would be deemed
insane themselves. Finally, they brought in the family doctor
who had known the man his whole life. The doctor asked
him whether dead men bleed, to which the man replied no.
The doctor negotiated to make a small cut on the man's arm,
and to no one's surprise, the man bled from the incision. The
man's wife, family, and friends were relieved, for finally, they'd
proved the man was not dead. As they opened the door for
the family doctor to leave, the man replied: "I see I was wrong
... dead men, do bleed."[2]

The polarized position the fable's protagonist takes, denying perceived facts while only supporting preexisting belief,
seems ever more present today. Even in the process of being
proven wrong, he becomes more convinced of being right. We

see this "stuckness" in relationships, family, faith communities, organizations, politics, and countries, as well as the mass media. Society has moved to an either/or framework with little tolerance for the gray spaces between opposites. The either/or fallacy is a false dichotomy, a false belief greatly minimizing the possibility for alternative thought and action. Addressing the challenges of leadership demands a different approach.

Today, it seems, this either/or approach is more acute than ever before. For today's leaders, your skill in addressing and dealing with these symptoms has become ever more critical to your success.

It is easy to get drawn into the anxiety of the "dead person" and end up arguing or fighting with them or alienating them, abandoning them. In other words, taking up one of the two reptilian responses, fight or flight. As a leader, leading an organization, church, family, community, neither of these reptilian responses will result in a good outcome for anyone.

How would you respond to the "dead man" in the parable? Or, if we extend the parable, how would you engage the "dead" organization, the organization in gridlock; that is on the wrong path, but feeling secure with the path; the organization highly anxious and reactive rather than being high functioning and creative in its problem-solving? How you respond to these kinds of either/or situations says much about you, as a person, a "self".

Effective leadership = transformation and change

As a leader you manage and give direction to a team, a department, an institution, or a corporation. You lead others. This obvious fact, however, is a half-truth at best. In reality, one manages and leads one's *self* first before one leads *others*.

This book seeks to empower you to be a reflexive, self-aware person and partner who can lead with less anxiety, increased confidence, and a presence inviting others to follow you into change.

The paradox—leadership as leading self *and* leading others—easily becomes a problem when a leader is unaware of how their life story, personality, strengths, and weaknesses direct and affect every aspect of their leadership. You learned how to be in a relationship, also how to respond in moments of anxiety and manipulation, long before you even imagined being a leader. Your current leadership and relationship with co-workers are intricately tied to the system and relationships that welcomed you into this world and nurtured you to adulthood. You may find yourself dancing an intricate dance with those around you. With some in your system, you seem naturally in step. *Why?* In your dance with others, you are continually stepping on toes, or it feels as if you are being stepped upon, dancing to a foreign tune. *Why?* You know certain conversations need to take place, but the challenging issues are being avoided. *Why? What would it take for you and those around you to find a rhythm that can overcome challenges and open new possibilities for your team or institution?* As a leader, you cannot detach yourself from those around you and believe they will allow you to manage, facilitate, and lead. Rather, someone, likely the person carrying the highest levels of anxiety, will step into the void created when you do not show up to be a leader. Suddenly you receive suggestions on how best to proceed; you are reminded by a person who states they have your best interests in mind, but some co-workers are unhappy and are thwarting change. It's much like one sibling telling on another to get a parent's attention.

Excellent leaders embrace paradox

Paradoxes cannot be solved. Rather, they introduce tension best held. Some leaders would rather turn the paradox into a dichotomy, an either/or tension, choosing one polarity over the other. They believe they are good at leading others even when they neglect personal relationships, their professional goals, and their holistic well-being. They fool themselves by thinking they can lead others after they have given up on working to become better versions of themselves. Increasingly, leaders rely on data to bridge the paradox of leadership and in their search for excellence. Data, we'll argue, fail miserably in this regard and expose anxious, ineffectual leadership. Other leaders yet focus all their attention on the task at hand, losing sight of a larger vision. Worse yet, other leaders focus all their attention and resources on a minor issue of little importance, a dynamic called selective abstraction. And then there are the leaders who show up with such force any energy or vitality in a room seems to disappear as people fall into silence, sheepishly following their unquestionable, charismatic leader. These approaches to leadership and managing anxiety, which we are convinced you have witnessed, are problematic and promise only failure.

The Essence of Leadership offers a framework—family systems theory—to unpack the dynamics found in offices around the world. The book shows you ways to be an effective leader leading differently, but with confidence and success. Every leader is tasked to bring change but finds themselves in a system resisting the very change that is in their charge. This, we believe, is your world too.

One can make the argument that families and later clans were the first "organizations" to be formed and required the first leaders to appear. Negotiating family dynamics predates, by millennia, anything we've learned about relationships and leadership from faith communities, companies, businesses, universities, and institutions. It should not surprise us that our responses to the environment and to others are very much shaped by the assimilation processes within a family or perceived family, or the lack thereof. The roles and functions a person assumes in life, as well as the position they take within systems of power, are greatly defined, either explicitly or implicitly, by the experiences they had in their family of origin. We may need a reminder that, before organizational charts, human resource departments, and consultants with PowerPoint slides, families and clans have been and remain the bedrock of how humans organize to survive, thrive, and expand.

We are individuals who uniquely crave relational and leadership approaches in life. The relationships formed between partners, parents, and children greatly define how we interact with people and things, for good and for ill. Family behavior patterns are formed before birth and accelerate the first years of a child's life. These patterns are deeply rooted in us all, due to, if nothing else, the frequency of interactions and practice, but also because these behaviors are instilled in unconscious ways, creating a muscle memory reflex, of sorts. Furthermore, the emotional process within families can span generations and is basic to all organizational structures and professional relationships.

Families understood the benefits of working together to survive, thrive, and expand. This resulted in families becoming clans or tribes of various sizes and to various levels of sophistication and success. Family expanded beyond blood relations to include one's chosen family. As the family had to integrate into larger systems, it required different forms, roles, and functions not based on blood relations, parental rights, or birth order. Systems became more complex, perhaps based on the nature of a relationship, skills, knowledge, wisdom, strength, health, competitiveness, age, or a value such as care or compassion. The clans, as various family units committed to each other, expanded and developed organizational structures and new rules and principles so they could function effectively. Often tribes would get too big and would splinter into smaller clans.

Just as families have their moments of joy, they have their moments of conflict. How they manage conflict, in particular, will define their likely chance of long-term success and their ability to stay intact. Tribes are a large family made up of smaller families, with the same challenges and conflicts. The larger the tribe, the more complex it is to manage and the more challenging it is for the leader to lead effectively.

For many adults in the West, institutions, organizations, small businesses, and corporations—those entities employing most workers—have replaced families as their primary relational context. These institutions have organizational charts alongside human resource and finance departments. Still, we find ourselves members of institutions formed by persons where relational patterns mimic those patterns we first encountered in our families of origin. There is a peculiar familiarity, one that often remains mostly unconscious, with family characteristics and principles we have all learned from a young age and repeated over generations, manifesting around us as employees and employers. As children, we grow up in our families and then go off to work in companies. These organizations and companies, we hope, are led by appointed leaders who can navigate the same relationship dynamics we first encountered in our families, but on a much larger scale and with a deeper complexity. Since organizations and companies are a collection of families and families have problems, companies too have problems, and lots of them. If you reflect on how many challenges there are in your family, multiply that by a few thousand and you get a company.

A key skill then for modern-day leaders is how to manage these very large, very complex families and to do this at ever-increasing speeds with ever-lower tolerances for mistakes of any kind.

Addressing Difficulties, Preventing Problems

Communication theorists Paul Watzlawick, John Weakland, and Richard Fisch write in their book *Change: Principles of Problem Formation and Problem Resolution* that problems are difficulties that become exacerbated to the point they now demand many resources to address, *if* they can even be addressed.[3] The authors distinguish between *difficulties* and *problems.* Whereas difficulties are "an undesirable state of affairs which [...] can be resolved through some common-sense action ... Problems [refer to] impasses, deadlocks, knots, etc." Leaders who either take no action, take action when none is needed, or take the wrong action turn difficulties into problems and get their communities stuck. Effective leaders thus distinguish difficulties from problems, do not let difficulties become problems, and know how best to address a difficult situation or one becoming a problem. This, of course, is easier said than done. As a leader this task becomes easier if you know your strengths and weaknesses, when you can recognize how you are part of a system, and when you seek to be responsive and not reactive in moments of anxiety. Simply put, essential leaders prohibit the inevitable difficulties of organizational or corporate life from becoming problems.

We're reminded of a leadership team that resisted our recommendation to function more effectively as a team and empower middle management. The leadership opted for a new logo, new office furniture, and a new paint color—at great cost—to boost the perceived lack of morale between staff members and to improve the organization's outward image to reflect a modern corporation. The business was burdened by the additional financial strain while staff members, fearing they would be let go as part of cost-savings measures, resigned and sought more secure employment. In a different organization, the CEO allowed two senior members of his leadership team to engage in open hostility. The senior leaders demeaned each other in professional contexts and many in the industry knew about their intense dislike of each other. The hostility caused much anxiety among junior members of the leadership team. In fear of retribution, junior members rarely contributed to decisions made. The hostility disappeared due to a retirement, but years of conflict left a culture where differences became anxiety-filled chasms, best left unaddressed.

We have, of course, met excellent, responsive leaders. Zach is the director of a housing nonprofit covering multiple states. He has been very successful in landing grants and loans to build affordable housing units for housing-insecure persons. Zach spends most of his time empowering his six-person leadership team. They have become the public face of the organization, with Zach rarely seeking the limelight. Across the city, Zach mentors numerous nonprofit leaders outside his organization. He exudes a nonthreatened, confident presence. Zach's office is one of the smallest in their administrative building but often frequented. As a housing bubble gripped much of the United States, Zach's Board of Directors became increasingly anxious. Some wondered where they will find affordable properties to develop. Other members lamented how political forces influence grant possibilities. Other board members yet stated the nonprofit should sell some of its properties to cash in on the high property values. That many would lose the place they call home did not seem to bother those members. Zach became a buffer between the nonprofit's key stakeholders—persons who are housing-insecure—and the board. Few outside Zach's core leadership team knew about the tensions he faced. Zach's sense of inner peace seems unfazed by the inevitable challenges his nonprofit faces. Not surprisingly, the housing nonprofit Zach leads experiences little staff turnover and is a sought-after internship site for students. *What is different about Zach and his leadership compared to the leaders who focused their teams' attention on the wrong place or who allowed open hostility among senior leaders to grow?*

Effective leaders are responsive to difficulties

You have witnessed leaders, teams, and institutions stuck as difficulties became problems. You have also witnessed effective leadership. Think of the leader:

- who is so beholden to stakeholders that they alienate their workforce;
- who remains responsive and open to change;
- who is on a path of burnout;
- who dances effortlessly with various stakeholders;
- who walks the high moral ground, only to get caught in some ethical controversy;
- who embraces the anxiety change initiates;
- who fails to admit wrongdoing or mistakes made;
- who is transparent about how decisions are made;
- who denies the emotional and relational components of leadership and instead focuses only on rational analysis, or the leader who is deeply empathic and trustworthy;
- who is a buffer between a board's anxiety and the staff;
- who tries to bring stability to the company while allowing personal and familial tensions to grow;
- who sees constant declines yet refuses to try something different;
- who mindfully initiates and oversees transformation;
- whose poor communication undermines the change sought;
- who remains responsive and open to change with the deep awareness that all change is experienced as loss;
- who is risk averse and now frustrates or denies exciting possibilities;
- who is secure enough to invite differences of opinion;
- who forces their way in life;
- who experiences a deep sense of leadership satisfaction.

No doubt you have witnessed many kinds of leadership. Every leader, however, has to engage the emotional processes in the systems they are a part of. *What kind of leader do you hope to be? What needs to change in you and in your leadership practices for you to become a confident, recognized leader?* We argue that you need to know about the traits leaders' share, while remaining responsive to the emotional reactions found in every system.

Leadership Defined

Essential leadership holds a paradox: one must lead oneself before one can lead others. This is not a problem to be fixed, but rather a possibility to embrace. You have much control over managing your self, which makes leading others an easier task. *Where in your leadership have you effectively managed yourself or facilitated change in the face of resistance? How did you manage to remain less anxious and facilitate trans- formation? What default reactions of leadership did you have to bracket or acknowledge, for they would not have served you well? How would you feel about yourself if you replicated this moment in your leadership more often?*

When a leader deepens their self-understanding and increases their mindfulness—aspects of self-differentiation we'll explore later—their leadership becomes filled with promise. Because systems resist change, systems hold on to the myth that there is such a thing as a natural leader, for in doing so they guarantee the system will remain unchanged.

We've used the term *leadership* several times already without defining it. Such is the power of words like "leader," "lead-ing," and "leadership." As a society, we've been enculturated into having a rather clear image in our minds of who a leader should be and what leadership is. Our definition of leadership is informed by family systems theory:

Leadership is mastering an emotional and relational process within a system while seeking to bring change according to clearly defined goals and ethical principles. Leadership relies on the leader's self as well as the leader's ability to engage their system.
Simply put, a leader is someone who invests in persons, communities, and processes to deliver an ethical and needed change.

Leadership is mastering an emotional and relational process

Let's unpack this definition. "Mastering," especially in the West, brings connotations of conquering, controlling, having power over, overcoming, and even subduing. It can also mean learning, understanding, or grasping. Here, *mastering* embraces the latter understandings and resists any connotation of power over. For us, mastering implies recognizing, engaging, learning about, and responding to the emotional process within a system, an uncontrollable process, but it can be joined and indirectly influenced through one's actions. As one grows in mastering the emotional process, one's respect for its presence and power increases.

"Emotional," in turn, indicates automatic human responses, the unconscious legacy of our evolutionary journey to becoming *homo sapiens*. These responses increase when we feel change is coming or when we perceive ourselves to be under imagined or real threat. We humans almost always experience change as a threat. The "emotional process" thus describes the emotional "energy" (on a personal level we may call it "chemistry") flowing between people and within a system as the system faces change. Since the only entity without anxiety is a dead entity, excellent leaders are never nonanxious leaders. Rather, leaders have vitality, an energy akin to a healthy dose of anxiety. Essential leaders portray less of the resistant, defensive, passive, and manipulative anxiety or energy, leaving a system unchanged amidst dysfunction and conflict.

A "system" is all persons and things making a team or an institution, including all its people, processes, resources, vision and mission statements, and even hopes and dreams. The various elements in a system are in constant relationship with each other, which is naturally reactive, but with mindfulness can become responsive, i.e., can be addressed with mindful discernment. The relationships of the various parts within a system are not hierarchical. Someone low on the organizational chart can have much power over whether a system works or not. In a hospital system, for example, a custodian who needs to clean a hospital room to ready it for a new patient holds much power. The custodian is slow to show up and cleans at a similar pace. The Chief of Staff or Nursing Director, seeking to find a bed for a patient, is beholden to the speed and quality of cleaning by the custodial staff. The different elements of a system continually communicate with each other, sometimes consciously and overtly, but most often in ways not easily recognized. *What might the slow custodian be communicating to the hospital's leadership?*

Our definition of leadership is informed by Rabbi Edwin Friedman, a family therapist and renowned leadership consultant, who sees leadership essentially being "an emotional process rather than a cognitive phenomenon, and [includes the] importance of well-differentiated leadership for the functioning and survival of institutions."[4] Since leadership seeks a greater good, there is a therapeutic modality to leadership, which should not be confused with the leader being a therapist.

So, who is a leader?

> *A leader is someone who creates space for a particular community to grow or embrace change, reaching explicit goals despite inherent anxiety and resistance.*

A leader creates space for change

Simply put, a leader is someone who invests in persons, communities, and processes to bring about mutually agreed-upon change.

How one measures the effectiveness of a leader shifts if the quality of emotional and relational systems, as the core of any institution, is accepted as criteria. Effectiveness can no longer be measured by being popular, by money, by power, or even by recognition. All these perceived wins are possible without the emotional process changing in any way, which implies the change will be short-lived. We know several "turnaround" experts, leaders who join an organization becoming a "sinking ship." They are called upon to make the company presentable, and then sell it to another company as a profitable enterprise. These experts are successful at what they do and do manage to get top dollar for previously strained businesses. Their short-term engagement, usually two to five years, however, almost always leaves the emotional process of the once "sinking ship" untouched, even if many employees are fired or choose to leave. The merged company is in immediate trouble. It's no surprise more than 70% of mergers fail.[5] To build long-term success, leaders cannot ignore the emotional processes in their institutions, or at least not for very long. Changing the emotional process might be the intangible but true value of a turnaround company.

One turnaround leader's first step, recognizing the impact of the emotional process, is to hold meetings with individual board and executive team members, then round-the-clock meetings with shift managers and employees. Key performance metrics are studied beforehand, but through engagement, 80% of the turnaround plan is provided by the existing board, executives, managers, and staff, who had not previously been asked to speak and offer solutions. By removing fear of retribution, this leader and their team engage the emotional processes within a company, rather than cramming down an approach. Not surprisingly, this firm is highly successful.

There is a "more than" quality to leadership, and it is this quality we explore. Leadership is more than being charismatic, for example. It is more than being able to cast a compelling vision or wielding a lot of power. Essential leadership does not discriminate: regardless of one's gender, race, class, sexual orientation, age, and ability, one can be a transformational leader. We decry and resist systems in which power structures keep transformational leaders from being recognized or systems elevating persons with little experience and without the necessary support systems to succeed. There are ways to overcome prejudice: those who hire employees or team members can create a blind process in which the resumé, the candidate's visual presentation, and their voice are masked to ensure the best person can be chosen for the position, minimizing biases and stereotypes. The best person, inevitably, will be someone who can engage in the emotional process they will enter.

In *The Essence of Leadership*, we suggest three "more than" qualities for being a leader:

1. Leaders engage and manage their own emotional and relational worlds.
2. They master the emotional processes of the system(s) of which they are a part.
3. Leaders are responsive to both the past and the present in ways that unfold a changed future for a system.

Drawing on sociologist Clifford Geertz, we see these three broad criteria as "thick" descriptions of leadership and the tasks of leadership, which are not easily understood or defined because they contain subjective and even liminal components and are part of a rich context.[6] A "thick" description is often used in the social sciences to take persons, their subjectivity and behavior, and their contexts into consideration. It describes a holistic-as-possible look at situations. "Thin" descriptions would be superficial descriptions. We believe systems theory, complemented by a psychodynamic understanding of the person of a leader, brings much to an exploration of leadership.

Leadership is often dangerous to one's health. Physicians, a population we work with closely, face alarmingly high levels of burnout, depression, and suicide, far exceeding the general population.[7] With physicians being at the forefront of our society's healthcare, physician well-being can be seen as a refined lens into societal dysfunction. Physician well-being reflects not only sources of pain and despair but reveals a leadership crisis. Humans can only shoulder so much burden and stay quiet when many new concepts, untested, might either enhance or crush the processes of families, organizations, and society. The COVID-19 pandemic accentuated the importance of the holistic health of all care providers. We do not think physicians are unique in this, for maintaining health and a healthy workplace culture are challenges every leader faces.

An Emotional Challenge

Leaders receive many versions of "No, I do not support this change" before a "Yes, I will follow you into change" is heard. We need to heed researchers who found we need five positive interactions or experiences to combat a single negative one.[8] Every leader experiences negative, challenging, stress-inducing experiences. When they do experience a positive "win," it is but a fleeting moment. *The Essence of Leadership* accepts all leadership is emotional first, and negative, frustrating, and painful experiences stay with us much longer than positive ones. When a leader can mindfully reposition themselves vis-à-vis the stress and anxiety in a system, their emotional and physical health improves, and coping mechanisms such as destructive self-medication diminish.[9] Still, leaders must maintain objective courage, based on valid academic research into personal, family, societal, economic, and leadership realities, to chart a path with their team or for their organization. To do otherwise, meaning to be led to and from emotion and relational perspectives solely, as we'll explore, will spell disaster.

Effective leaders manage stress and disappointment well. They also create deliberate dissatisfaction which induces anxiety in their systems. It's worth stating again: *Effective leaders deliberately create dissatisfaction and induce anxiety in their systems.* This is an especially difficult realization and task as many leaders prefer to avoid conflict and anxiety, work hard to keep opposing parties happy, and have a deep need to be liked. Creating dissatisfaction by critically engaging one's system, as we'll explore, does not gel easily with the natural dispositions of these leaders (see Chapter 1). To be clear, inducing anxiety can be done in numerous ways, some deeply dysfunctional. Here we imply anxiety increasing due to deliberate responsiveness to the emotional process in a system. In the following chapters, this statement will become clear. Certainly, anxiety can be raised in many questionable ways, often foregoing collaborative discernment: letting go of key personnel and staff; dissolving the board of directors; buying or selling a new business; introducing new, arbitrary protocols; announcing new and unproven partnerships, and more. Not all anxieties are equal. Some tensions and anxieties will paralyze a system, while others are crucial as catalysts of change. Engaging in the emotional process will cause dissatisfaction. It is needed to dislodge a system or institution from its current position and to embrace change.

Anticipation

How can this book be received? What are its purposes and aims? Expectations, after all, are key to personal flourishing, leadership satisfaction, and effective change. We begin with what this book is not.

First, *The Essence of Leadership* is not a self-help, "how to …" book, even as we encourage you to grow in specific ways and offer specific leadership practices. It is highly unlikely you will read this book and see immediate results in your leadership. This is not a despairing comment but we believe most often the best change comes in small steps over time. If leading self and managing others were as easy as reading a book, excellent leadership would not be as elusive as it is. We are confident in what we invite you to. You can expect that your self-awareness and understanding of how systems function will be affirmed and grow, which will change the way you lead. You can trust those changes since they are backed by significant empirical research across various spheres of life, from the personal to the familial, and from the therapeutic and the classroom, the boardroom, and the team meeting. No doubt this book will empower you to survey you being a leader. It will show ways how to grow in incremental ways along a seasoned path. Above all, you will be challenged to be true to yourself and at the same time be authentic toward your team or employer.

Second, this is not a book filled with the latest empirical research and data in support of our arguments. The book is grounded in the core theory that has evolved over the past 70 years. Significant empirical research on the theory and its use in leadership is readily available through a simple online search of reputable journals. We certainly point to key theorists and do quote research, but this book is qualitative and analytic in nature; it is not an empirical study of leadership.

Data-driven leadership, important today, looks different for a differentiated leader as they engage the system's emotional process and refrain from using data as the primary mechanism to induce change.

Third, this book does not aim to create a new theory of leadership. Rather, we draw on a way of understanding individuals within systems widely used in therapeutic contexts and leadership formation. You can rightly ask: *Why have you not written a groundbreaking book that offers five keys to unlock leadership? Why should I read it?* The short answer is we have never found a book offering five keys to leadership as truly transformative or enduring. We have found the "emotional" nature of family systems theory remains underexplored for executive leadership because Main Street defines leadership most often in terms of being a visionary, charismatic, transactional leader-as-entrepreneur. Our proposed model of leadership can be refreshingly embraced by many leaders, regardless of the size of their organization or where they find themselves in the hierarchy within their institutions. Many leaders crave a better way as the burden of their learned traditional approach to leadership cannot be sustained. We believe the combination of systems thinking, psychodynamic insights (about the self of the leader), and having select analytical tools to inform one's decision-making *is* filled with possibilities. Twenty or 30 years from now, if not a 1000 years from now, the need for self-differentiated leaders will not only remain, but we expect it to be needed more than ever.

Reading this book is going to help you become a vision *catcher*—discovering a vision through communal discernment as someone who can read emotional processes—not only a vision *caster*. Though society idealizes vision casters—Henry Ford, Steve Jobs, Elon Musk, Bill Gates, Sam Walton, Jack Ma, Ma Huateng, Tony Zhang, Oprah Winfrey, Meg Whitman, Marisa Myers, Beyoncé, and Arianna Huffington, to name a few, and maybe for good reasons—we are interested in self-differentiated leadership as an open invitation to every person who manages others.

So what can we claim positively about our book's goals? *The Essence of Leadership* will empower you to be a differentiated leader, someone who can engage your own personal and relational processes even as you can engage those same processes in the professional systems you find themselves a part of. If you find yourself stuck in your interpersonal life, your chances are greatly diminished of finding optimal relationships and efficiency in the workplace. A leader who cannot address conflict in their intimate relationships is less likely to facilitate difficult conversations in their team. A leader who is shame-prone will personalize challenges made to their professional authority and will rarely apologize for mistakes made. Leaders who are differentiated are sought-after as people naturally gravitate to those who thrive in systems where others flounder, as we'll discuss.

Since we begin with you as a person before you are a leader, this book seeks to empower you to be a creative and ethical person, a more loving and caring partner and parent (or someone engaging the current, younger generation), and an effective leader. Maybe this goal is reason enough to read the book. We want to facilitate the possibility for you to flourish. If you bring your growing and changing self to your leadership, expect positive results.

Lastly, *The Essence of Leadership* seeks to empower you as a change agent. No leader is asked to lead only to maintain the status quo. Since change permeates all of reality, every attempt to maintain the status quo will fail. But, as we said, change is always resisted; being a change agent is no simple task. Since you can expect change and deeper awareness in yourself through the engagement of this book, you can rightly expect changes in your personal life and as a professional.

Leaders are change agents

This book, we believe, is best read as an invitation to embark on a path of slow, but deliberate transformation. As such, we wrote it to be welcoming, digestible, and with pointers to deeper theory and sources should that spark your interest. The case studies we use are never about one individual but describe leaders and situations we've encountered. And though our work environments are higher education, not-for-profit corporations, the healthcare industry, and the corporate-for-profit industrial complex, we think the principles of leadership we explore apply to every leader seeking to facilitate change, regardless of a leader's context, role, or function.

We recommend you read this book with the mindset of being transformed, even if the change or growth will be slow and incremental. Highlight or note whatever resonates with you and whatever provokes questions in you; take your thoughts to mentors, colleagues, and friends; and finally, return to those insights or questions over time to allow deeper personal integration of what you are learning. Teams and cohort leaders will benefit from reading the book together and discussing its contents. We find this collaborative exploration important. It was central to the ways we wrote the book. Resist being a leader who overhears a new approach and immediately seeks to implement what they have heard. Nature tells us slow growth is most often durable, sustainable growth. Allow the concepts of this book to become part of who you are. Spend some time noticing dynamics in you, in your relationships with loved ones and family, and in the leaders around you. Do so not to change others or conversations but to gain a deeper appreciation for family systems theory and to transform who you are in the different roles and functions you have. By leading differently, change will surprise you.

As you read this book, ask often: *Who am I as a leader? Who am I becoming? What might the leader I witness experience? What is happening here? What should be happening but is circumvented? What would I do differently? What does responsive leadership look like?* Once you have developed some confidence that you have integrated core concepts into your person, then leading differently will be a natural result. You will lead with authenticity, for how you lead will come from deep within you and will be part of you. It will no longer be an insight or technique or theory you read about, but you have become a different leader.

The next chapters address three core elements of essential leadership: the leader engaging and managing their own emotional and relational worlds, the leader next engaging the emotional processes of the system(s) of which they are a part, and the leader then being responsive to both the past and the present in ways unfolding a changed future for a system.

Notes

1. Edwin H. Friedman, *Friedman's Fables* (New York: Guilford Publications, 1990), 55. The fable is called "The Power of Belief."
2. Ibid., 58.
3. Paul Watzlawick, John H. Weakland, and Richard Fisch, *Change: Principles of Problem Formation and Problem Resolution* (New York: Norton, 1974), 38.
4. Edwin H. Friedman, *A Failure of Nerve: Leadership in the Age of the Quick Fix* (New York: Seabury Books, 2007), 31. Friedman draws on the work of psychiatrist Murray Bowen.
5. As quoted in the Harvard Business Review. See: https://hbr.org /2000/05/cracking-the-code-of-change. Accessed August 13, 2021.
6. Clifford Geertz, *The Interpretation of Cultures: Selected Essays* (London: Hutchinson, 1975), 6. Geertz, in turn, followed the British Philosopher Gilbert Ryle who distinguished "thin" versus "thick" descriptions as early as 1949.

7. See Amanda M. Kingston, "Break the Silence: Physician Suicide in the Time of Covid-19," *Missouri medicine* 117, no. 5 (2020); Tait D. Shanafelt and John H. Noseworthy, "Executive Leadership and Physician Well-Being: Nine Organizational Strategies to Promote Engagement and Reduce Burnout," *Mayo Clinic Proceedings* 92, no. 1 (January 2017): 129–46.

8. See John M. Gottman and Robert W. Levenson, "Marital Processes Predictive of Later Dissolution: Behavior, Physiology, and Health," *Journal of Personality and Social Psychology* 63, no. 2 (1992): 232.

9. For research indicating the relationship between self-differentiation, managing stress, and health, see Trevor J. Buser, Terry L. Pertuit, and Daniella L. Muller, "Nonsuicidal Self-Injury, Stress, and Self-Differentiation," *Adultspan Journal* 18, no. 1 (2019); Peter J. Jankowski and Lisa M. Hooper, "Differentiation of Self: A Validation Study of the Bowen Theory Construct," *Couple and Family Psychology: Research and Practice* 1, no. 3 (2012): 226.

LEADERS AND SYSTEMS

Chapter 1

Being a Self: Owning One's Emotions, Actions, and Potential

You bring yourself to your leadership. Despite leaders often finding themselves in full view of others, they rarely contemplate their selves, as if one can lead without a self. *"The Self,"* philosopher John McMurray writes, *"can be agent only by being also subject."*[1] McMurray reminds us doing something— being an agent—is determined by being someone—a subject. These unassuming and obvious statements imply that before achieving anything in your leadership you are someone with a unique life history, specific personality traits, characteristics, habits, relational capacities, a certain temperament, life skills, and more. Education, training, mentoring, and experience do influence who we are and how we lead, but less than imagined. In anxious moments we are likely to revert to our default nature. When a leader needs to be their best and others anticipate excellence, a leader often presents their unrefined, natural self.

DOI: 10.4324/9781003463993-3   **25**

The book's first two chapters focus on *being* someone before one is *doing* something. Whereas systems theory helps us understand how individuals within an organization relate to each other, psychology and psychodynamic theory give us insight into the person of a leader and as such complements systems theory. Of course, our personal and professional lives cannot be easily separated, as we'll explore. No doubt you have witnessed someone's leadership derail due to their personality traits, dispositions, or ethical choices, with lingering detrimental effects to the system even after they left. *At the heart of leadership lies the reflexive, mindful self.* Since you bring your self to your leadership, you intuitively know tending and regulating your self is the most basic leadership skill you have. Some leaders might argue who they are and their personal lives have nothing to do with who they are as leaders. They are wrong. They are also defensive in ways that inhibit their leadership. How one lives, loves, and works are deeply intertwined. The only constant in all areas of living is *you*—as a person, a partner, possibly a parent, and as a professional.

The Lives We Live

Dr. Ivan Smith is a department chair in a large hospital. He is a recognized physician loved by his patients. When he was appointed as chair, no one was surprised. Now, not even a year into his position as chair, he feels burdened by the stress tied to his position. First, he searched for and appointed numerous clinicians after a good number of his staff joined a rival institution in the same city. He underestimated the time, money, and challenges in hiring competent clinicians, each one coming with their own lists of expectations, including bringing their nursing and administrative staff with them. Dr. Smith's hiring of clinical staff has grown beyond recognition.

Adding to his stress is his own clinic functioning poorly. His staff are frustrated. The dissatisfaction has prompted some to leave and patient reviews remain critical of the service and care they received. Dr. Smith and his physician colleagues chart late into the night, adding to the frustration felt. The nursing staff feel caught between the patients and their care providers. A recent staff meeting ended in chaos as nurses, physicians, and the administrative staff blamed each other for the clinic's problems. Dr. Smith's statement—"Many times patients are not prepared to be seen by a doctor"—was met with much resistance and challenge from the nursing staff. Feeling the pushback, he became defensive and restated his comment, only to receive more intense pushback. Shortly after this meeting, which he later described as "disastrous" to a colleague, his tension increased in a meeting of department chairs where he learned the hospital's governing board would be announcing an expected 9% growth in revenue from each department for the upcoming financial year. Dr. Smith knows his clinic, which shows a slight decline year-over-year, is unlikely to reach the new financial goal. As a sense of failure grows in him, anger and cynicism cover a deeper sense of shame at the way things are unfolding.

At home, Dr. Smith finds it hard to relax and unwind. His teenage daughter was caught with marijuana at her private school. Though the school was lenient and only brought demerits and four weeks of "Saturday school," it heightened the tension in his home. Oscillating between stress, feeling incompetent and overwhelmed, and being tired, Dr. Smith finds some relief in drinking whisky when he retires to his home office. Sleep has become elusive despite his exhaustion. A recent night left his family numb when he wanted to pour himself another drink only to find empty bottles. He accused his daughter of drinking some of his whisky, which she vehemently denied. After a yelling match between dad and daughter, with mom a silent witness, Dr. Smith retreated to his office as his daughter got into her car and drove off.

Dr. Smith feels alone in this world, but his experience is shared by many.

Prof. Lindie Ludouw, a renowned dementia expert, knows different-yet-similar stress in the interweaving of her personal and professional lives. Care providers and counselors widely use her work and assessment tools. Her *Institute for Dementia in the Elderly* is a leader in the field. For many years, she managed to get grant funding to buy out some of her clinical hours, overseeing her Institute while seeing patients at a quarter clinical load. Unable to secure grants the last few years, she started seeing patients at a half load. This shift is both a loss and frustration. Her time at the Institute has greatly diminished and everything feels adrift. Her research has slowed down considerably as her clinical work inevitably takes her beyond dementia care, her primary interest. Since scaling back her time at the Institute as well as her research, she has published less and has received fewer invitations to speak at conferences.

For the past months, debilitating migraine headaches have plagued her. Reluctantly, she sought out a physician colleague, and their joint discernment was that the stress she is experiencing is increasing the intensity of her migraines. Thoughts of burnout have crossed her mind as she admits she is in a "bad" spot. Is she still the leader and researcher she and others thought she was? She certainly does not feel worthy of her past accomplishments. Besides medication, the best approach for her migraines is to rest and sleep. Prof. Ludouw's partner has been accommodating as she turns in early but has grown frustrated with the lack of intimacy in their relationship. Intimacy is now fused with caregiving as the migraine headaches have become a third party in their relationship.

These fictitious cases, built around conversations we've had with many leaders in the healthcare industry, speak to challenges all leaders face: *How does one lead in a highly competitive world where financial growth and near-perfect patient evaluations are expected? Where within a specialized career are leadership skills and business acumen acquired? How does one attain the "softer skills" of life, such as sustaining difficult conversations or being aware of emotional and relational worlds? What happens to leaders, personally and professionally, who lack those "softer skills"? In what ways does one's vocational stress enter one's body or the home one creates with a partner and loved ones? Why do leaders tend to become defensive when challenged? How does one cope with shifts in leadership or professional roles and functions? How can leaders sustain themselves in the face of larger systemic dysfunction? At what point is the fatigue one feels burnout or even clinical depression? When will self-medicating a symptom become a problem in itself?* Irrespective of how you perceive your leadership and context, you will have to find answers to questions like these probing the intersections of your personal and professional lives.

Leading with Strengths *and* an Achilles' Heel

There are many assessment tools leaders can use to understand themselves better. Few of them are standardized (and some are frankly the fruit of pseudoscience). With non-standardized tests, one can expect to see differences in one's results for the same test as situations and experiences change. An assessment instrument such as *The Minnesota Multiphasic Personality Inventory* (MMPI), standardized over many iterations, offers a more trustworthy picture of one's personality. In standardized inventories one cannot do "poorly" or "ace" the test; it merely gives you a picture of who you are, a picture that will remain relatively constant over time and circumstance.

The MMPI was created by two professors at the University of Minnesota in 1943. It has been through four major revisions, the last being in 2008 (MMPI-2-RF), has been standardized on certain populations, like clergy, who share a similar profile to that of physicians, and is used around the world. The clinical language of the MMPI scales is not important for our discussion, but the MMPI does show us a "typical" profile of traits that leaders carry.[2,3,4]

Leaders:

- Are passionate persons.
- Carry a narcissistic trait.
- Offer a superlative self (or want to be seen as having it all together).
- Explore uncharted terrain (or do their own thing).
- Are driven by a desire for more.
- Are prone to psychosomatic symptoms.

Leaders carry these traits at levels much higher than the general population, who share some of these traits, but are unlikely to carry all of them as leaders often do. Within these traits, we find strengths and weaknesses a leader brings.

Leaders often ride an emotional roller coaster

Leaders Are Passionate Persons

Excellent leaders feel intensely. They are passionate about their beliefs, their leadership skills, and the vision they can realize for others. There is an energy leaders exude, a passion, which is also anxiety. One's passion can range from being weak to being obsessed—at which point the passion determines one's being. In terms of being passionate, a leader's MMPI score can be almost double that of an "average" person. The general population, of course, are passionate too—think of sports fans—but rarely at a level matching the passion leaders bring. Whereas a fan may channel their passion toward a specific team, a leader's passion covers almost all they do and seek to accomplish. An entrepreneurial leader, for instance, is unlikely to succeed if not passionate to the point of being almost obsessed. This passion drives leaders to work many more hours beyond the perceived 40-hour workweek.

Though passion serves a leader well, it holds a twofold challenge: First, others may not be as excited about the leader's ideas as the leader is. And second, leaders often experience emotions intensely, whether the emotions are empowering and invigorating or burdening and draining. When we leaders are happy or excited, we tend to be very happy or excited; when we feel misunderstood, not recognized, or even rejected, the emotion hits us with a hard blow and can be difficult to shake.

Imagine a leader bringing a new vision for change to their team. If the team receives it in a lukewarm manner, the leader can swing from great expectation to deep frustration in seconds. The leader then often repeats themselves, as if the team did not hear them the first time. Sometimes a leader will raise their voice, trying to rally for the vision, asking folks to be excited in ways they're simply not wired to feel. The leader may even claim power over others and make a unilateral decision over teams who have little to no buy-in. Other times the leader will retreat to their office and berate themselves for not presenting the new vision in a way the team could receive it. They will fault themselves for presenting their case poorly and rarely question the vision offered. We'll expand on the inner critic later.

Interpreting the responses of others is rarely a good measure for leaders to use. Dr. Smith feels the call to care and lead as deeply as he is experiencing the stress of a poorly functioning clinic and a distancing daughter. Prof. Ludouw feels her loss around doing research and teaching and the strain on her intimate life as strongly as she is energized by speaking at conferences or assisting frail elderly. *A certain burden of leadership is being on an emotional rollercoaster of sorts.* Emotionally, but also physically, it is very challenging to be up one moment, feeling great about how things are progressing, and down the next, as if things are falling apart.

Effective leaders regulate their emotions. Their highs are high, but not too high. They embrace their lows but do not allow the lows to determine their thoughts and actions. They seek out mentors and others who may not fit this leadership profile, and ask: *Why are others not excited about my idea? Should I be as upset as I am?* or *How should I interpret the responses I got?* Recognizing the level of emotion in their lives, differentiated leaders seek healthy outlets, not just consulting with trusted others but also moving their bodies through exercise, finding hobbies that energize them differently, and cultivating their imagination and creativity.

Knowing you are passionate is a strength affirming your leadership. Remaining mindful about how feeling deeply affects you and your leadership is essential.

Leaders often have high levels of self-confidence

Leaders Carry a Narcissistic Trait

Excellent leaders believe in themselves. It takes a certain person to say: "I will bring change to this system"; or "I can solve this problem"; or "I will lead us all into the promised land"; or "I..." Do you hear the "I" becoming louder and more prominent, reflecting a narcissistic quality? We are not saying leaders are narcissists—though a select few may be. Narcissistic leaders initiate chaos around them (which they rarely recognize), exploits people and systems, shows little or no empathy, and has a vulnerable or fragile self they constantly must defend or need others to defend. They rarely last long in leadership unless they surround themselves with like-minded enabling others seeking to climb the leadership ladder.

Here we are describing a *trait or a characteristic*, not a personality type (which carries a clinical diagnosis). We can think about this trait in terms of believing in oneself. Leading without conviction you are competent and can make a difference might be impossible. Every leader must believe in their potential to take people or an organization on a journey and facilitate change. Witnessing a leader who is plagued with self-doubt and insecurities is painful. Again, we are talking about a healthy dose of self-confidence, which is neither being egotistical, self-centered, selfish, nor being self-absorbed. The latter traits cannot hold personal and professional relationships together, whereas believing in oneself is necessary for leadership.

Believing in oneself too has an Achilles' heel. The edge or downside of having a well-developed narcissistic trait is shame. Shame is the painful feeling of being exposed; being made vulnerable, being uncovered and left unprotected; and feeling naked and being looked at by others. When guilt states: "I did something wrong," shame states: "I am wrong"; "I am not worthy of this position"; and "I should have seen this coming"; or "If others know the true me they will reject me." Shame-related experiences are described in terms of being embarrassed; humiliated or disgraced, or feeling inadequate. We describe it in terms of losing face, feeling ridiculed, being dishonored; and being made to feel or appear weak by someone stronger. Shame faults us for being incompetent.

When shamed, we cannot maintain eye contact. Shame triggers bodily responses we cannot control, such as blushing, sweating, an increased heart rate, and shortness of breath. Inevitably, shame leads to being thin-skinned and vulnerable to perceived emotional and relational slights and hurts. We protect ourselves against shame in a variety of ways: by claiming exploitative power and control over others; with depressiveness, arrogance, or aloofness; by becoming "loud" and overbearing; by distancing ourselves from people and issues; by living a rational life denying the emotional world; by becoming competitive and trying to win at all costs; and even by having a righteous attitude of being right and perceiving others as being wrong. Anger and rage—lashing out—are common defenses against shame, as anger and rage empower a disempowered self. When feeling shame deeply, the result of narcissistic elements in the self, one's anger and rage can become volatile, often volcanic, as it suddenly rages after a period of dormancy.

We imagine you have been in a meeting where a leader was challenged. A scenario like this one unfolded: The leader missed something, forgot something, or clearly made a mistake, and then someone challenged or called out the leader in the presence of the others. Maybe the sales results or budget clearly showed the business model was failing. Immediately an awkward silence set in. What should not have been said was said because it needed to be said, and now everyone awaits the leader's reaction. They know what is transpiring in the mind of their leader, for every person knows shame intimately. The leader feels blamed and tries to save face. Maybe the leader quiets or diminishes (shames) the dissenting voice or tries to change the topic to deflect everyone's attention. Some leaders will immediately say that the person who raised the challenge did not know all the facts and the challenge could therefore be disregarded. Rather than holding their shame, the leader shames someone else. Sometimes there might be a person in the room trying to save their leader by making unhelpful comments in defense of the leader. "Every company is facing challenging times, we are still above the curve," we hear. We have seen religious leaders calling for prayer or some spiritual or ethical value to interrupt and deflect attention from their shame. Whatever the move the leader makes, few of us will challenge the leader's move, having witnessed their reaction to the perceived challenge. At this point, the meeting has dissolved into a fruitless gathering of people. Best to end the meeting, regroup at a different time, and try again.

Of course, all of this could have been averted if the leader had responded: "You know, you are right. What I just said does not make sense." Or, "I apologize. I missed the boat on this one." Or: "We are facing serious financial problems and together we have to find a way out." When one is mindful of how self and systems work, no one needs to be blamed or shamed. The self can manage its shame-based reactivity. The system, in turn, does not function in a cause-and-effect manner, where someone can be blamed, but functions through relational connections and dynamics.

Effective leaders believe in themselves; they also remain mindful of the experience of shame and how one defends oneself against this painful intrapsychic experience. Such leaders imagine themselves in difficult moments and practice responses that are professional, ethical, and facilitate further conversation and discernment. They revisit past shaming experiences, possibly from childhood, and ask themselves when those experiences will surprise them in their leadership and how they will respond when it happens. They surround themselves with persons with whom they can process experiences—life coaches, counselors, mentors, and colleagues.

Not becoming defensive is a challenge for us leaders, for we carry another trait fueling our defensiveness: we want to be seen as being professional and competent. We want to present what is called a superlative, exceptional self. The intricate ways the leadership traits we identify are woven together are becoming more apparent.

Leaders can be defensive

Leaders Offer a Superlative Self

Leaders prefer to portray themselves as professionals who are competent, who can be trusted, as persons who have it all together. *Why would others appoint or follow a leader who presents as incompetent, untrustworthy, or incapable of leading a team or institution somewhere?* We'll give some answers to this question in the following chapters, as people do indeed follow incompetence. Having a superlative self-presentation shows your best side to people. Excellent leaders rarely air their dirty laundry in public unless their Achilles' heel catches them off guard. No, we project the image of the utmost professionalism, and as such that trait serves us well.

The trouble with having a self presenting as being totally "together" is threefold. First, it resists acknowledging those moments when one is lost or have some difficulties. Every leader faces such moments. Second, it keeps us from seeking help or advice, even empowering others. We do not want others to be more competent than us. And third, the superlative self wants to be liked by others and thus avoids moments of conflict and tension. Someone who fights with you does not appreciate you, a desire the superlative self has. Leading without moments of conflict and tension, of course, is impossible.

The superlative self easily becomes defensive when a leader feels challenged in three areas: Competence, belonging, and control. Competence: *Will people still see me as a great leader if I admit I have no clue how to respond next? What will people think of me if they discover I am struggling to reach my professional goals? Do I wear a power suit or expensive watch to project the image that I am a great leader? When will the person I mentor exceed me?* Belonging: *What if people notice my personal life has spilled over into my professional life? Will I be liked by others if I am authentic? Who will be my friends?* Control: *When a supervisor tasks me with something, am I being controlled? Am I losing control when I empower others to lead in ways different from the way I would lead? If I do not control every point of decision-making, will the vision for the institution I have come true?*

Effective leaders embrace the paradox that they project a professional, competent self *even as* they admit mistakes, seek help, and empower others to surpass them in leading. Leaders who differentiate themselves from other leaders have relationships, conversation partners, and settings where it would be appropriate to admit struggles, work through tensions, and discover new approaches to leadership. When defensiveness has become a go-to strategy for a leader under pressure, their leadership hopes will soon buckle under the weight of their superlative self.

A leader's sense of professionalism and competence is closely related to another trait common to leaders: venturing into uncharted terrain and risking something new.

Leaders are pathfinders

Leaders Explore Uncharted Terrain (or Do Their Own Thing)

Drawing on insights from the MMPI, thus far we have said leaders are passionate persons, they have a strong belief in themselves, and they present themselves in superlative, "always together" ways. A fourth trait leaders share is they readily explore new terrain, i.e., they do not turn away from change or trying something new. Furthermore, leaders prefer doing their own thing rather than following in the footsteps of others. As such, leaders thrive at casting new visions, bringing change, doing something new, and facilitating transformation. The tasks and expectations of leadership are challenging, especially as most leaders face the challenge of changing the status quo. Leaders carry visions of growth or a thriving organization, of paving a new way. A leader's desire to cut new paths may be a defining trait propelling people to follow a leader.

Like all strengths, however, doing one's own thing (even when inviting others along) can become a leader's Achilles' heel. Few leaders, even private business owners, do not "work" for someone else. As leaders, most often we simply cannot do our own thing. There are supervisors or direct reports who will co-determine decisions made or even provide the vision; there are boards who give direction but also hold leadership accountable; there is the supervision of public opinion; the validation by the market economy; the oversight of accreditation and financial institutions; there are always ethical and legal implications for one's leadership. Thus, as much as leaders want to do their own thing, they are always constrained by various stakeholder relationships. As leaders, we know we cannot always do what we want to do. No doubt you know a leader who flamed out of a position under a cloud of scandal because their professional path diverted from the institution or because their path took them over ethical or legal boundaries and crossed a governing board.

Effective leaders can walk the fine line between doing something new, continuing what was, and being accountable to various stakeholders. They can hold the tension when they must let go of their plan; when it feels as if they acquiesce to forces that are not only prescriptive but also inhibiting. Leaders who embrace the trait of doing their own thing and resisting following others stay in close conversation with teams, supervisors, boards, and regulatory agencies; they frequently seek input and complicate the discernment process. Successful leaders learn that restrictions and boundaries are needed to flourish in life and it's possible to be creative on a playground someone else designed.

Doing new things and being in exciting conversations inevitably bring tension to a leader. Managing this tension often determines one's longevity in leadership.

Leaders Are Driven by a Desire for More

Leaders typically feel there is more to be achieved. They have a desire or longing not easily met, a hunger of sorts. The MMPI indicates a person's proneness to addictive behaviors and attitudes. It recognizes an addictive trait, *a desire for more, of not being satisfied*, in leaders. This desire should not be confused with a clinical diagnosis of addiction. Leaders rely in subtle ways on this trait of desiring more. It keeps them in the game, constantly reminding them there is more to be accomplished, that one has not yet reached one's personal and professional goals. Keeping oneself in the game is important, especially when adversity sets in, which inevitably happens, or when goalposts begin to shift, which they always do. The dissatisfaction tied to this trait fuels determination, resilience, gumption, and grit. The desire for more is linked to our deeper quest for purpose and meaning, for what makes life worth living.

As with all the traits we've mentioned, this desire for more too can easily turn on a leader. Dr. Smith relies on alcohol to take the edge off his day. How long before he needs increased quantities to have the desired effect? Or worse, becomes an alcoholic? Food is an obvious choice for this trait and redefines the meaning of "hunger." One can become "addicted" to work. Some leaders remain hungry for excitement, which they will create through poor discernment, serving no one well, including themselves. Some leaders risk life and limb, literally running themselves into the ground. Or they seek thrills in speed, height, distance, sex, and more. Gambling, a play activity not unknown to leaders and executives, not only exposes the longing we identify here but also the self-belief one can beat the house. Pornography shows that taking in image after image rarely satisfies the underlying relational hunger for authentic intimacy as the brain bores without variety. Shopping or buying likewise can serve the hunger for more.

Wise leaders choose carefully how they feed the "hunger" in them. They recognize when the desire for more can cross personal, professional, and ethical boundaries. Regardless of the "substance" preferred to still this hunger for more—the anxiety in a system, food, alcohol, money, or images—the result is often the same: dissatisfaction and a depleted self. By contrast, leaders who pursue healthy habits—yoga, meditation, friendships, a hobby, volunteering, or exercise—are more likely to avoid the negative elements of having a hungry self.

Leaders want more

Leaders Are Prone to Psychosomatic Symptoms

One would think a bodily reaction, such as Prof. Ludouw's migraine headaches, is negative, and only negative. Not so. The MMPI, through a configuration called a "Conversion Valley," highlights the possibility of proneness to somatic symptoms. Between one's depressive trait, attempts at keeping up appearances (due to the superlative and defensive self), and anxiety (feeling intensely), the body experiences and manifests tension in somatic ways. Leaders who are not emotionally attuned to their bodies are especially prone to somatize.

Somatization is a positive response when a leader becomes curious about their symptom and discovers healthy ways to address the symptoms. Symptoms often communicate something is amiss in a system, and if we listen to that communication, they can be redeemed as a positive in our lives. We recommend a playful approach to symptoms while seeking out medical consultations. Prof. Ludouw, struggling with migraine headaches, might ask herself: "What is going against my grain? What is bugging me or is getting under my skin?" The leader with allergies can ask: "At what or whom do I want to thumb my nose?" A person with depression can ask: "What am I repressing? What is pressing on or in me?" Gastrointestinal concerns and acid reflux? Ask: "What can I not stomach?" Keeping weight on: "Of what can I not let go?" Feeling tired even when you get plenty of sleep? "What do I need to put to bed?" Premature ejaculation or erectile dysfunction? Ask: "What am I rushing toward? What anxiety is taking my power away?"

We certainly do not seek to minimize illness. Illness and pain are complex, and we do not suggest a linear relationship between illness and our emotional worlds. Rather, *we honor that the body is susceptible to the stresses and stressors we experience as leaders.* We accept that every illness has an emotional element. Being playful with our symptoms can bring not only insight into who we are and how we engage our professional and personal lives, but it can also bring relief by showing alternative and healthier ways to address the situations we face. Grieving the inherent losses within one's professional journey is a mature response and may alleviate the stress seeking to enter the body.

Stress and tension always enter one's body

The traits we highlighted as strengths and weaknesses provide a mirror in which you as a leader can grow your mindfulness (Table 1.1):

Table 1.1 Strengths and Weaknesses of Leaders

Recognize	Guard against
Passion	Feeling disappointed or rejected
Self-confidence and narcissistic traits	Shaming self and other; turning to shame defenses
A superlative self	Being defensive; resisting seeking help
The need to do one's own thing	Being a poor team member; Crossing ethical and other barriers
The desire for more	Pursuing compulsive and potentially addictive behaviors, Avoiding risky behavior
The body's symptoms	Listening poorly to the body's communications; self-medicating

You may not be able to recognize yourself in every trait we discussed, but we imagine you'll resonate with the majority of these. *A paradox of leadership is that one needs these traits to be excellent at leading others.* Granted, we may not need the last trait of embodying stress and anxiety, but that leaders can somatize is important and acts as a proverbial canary in the coal mine. Symptoms remind us we are embodied persons. Looking into the mirror we provide is an invitation to grow as a leader. Resist any other defensive interpretations.

Our inner dynamics, however, are complex and go deeper than the traits we have identified.

Leading from One of Three "Selves"

Psychology taught us we are a multiple self, debunking the belief in a unitary self. Ronald Fairbairn, a Scottish physician and psychiatrist (1889–1965), played a central role in this learning and helped us understand how the self develops in relationships with others.[5] Fairbairn remains an unexplored conversation partner for leadership development. His insights, however, can help leaders understand not only themselves but also those they lead. Fairbairn was one of the first theorists to explore the voice in our heads—which he called *the inner critic*. It is the voice reminding you after a presentation, a meeting, or a conversation about what you should have said or done but neglected to do. The inner critic always has the perfect comeback but shares its wisdom only after the fact. Fairbairn was an innovative theorist diverging from Sigmund Freud by saying that our deepest human drive and desire is the need to be in a relationship, with self, others, nature, and what is perceived as sacred. We seek a relationship with persons and things, said Fairbairn, and not with pleasure, as Freud argued.

The self has three distinct parts

Fairbairn described the self as having three distinct but interrelated parts, each part playing an important role in how life is experienced and lived (See Figure 1.1). The mentioned inner critic is one part. The three parts developed in early infancy as parental figures, thumbs, spoons, and also soft toys and blankets are internalized to become part of the self. The first part of the self has executive functions, which Fairbairn called the *central ego* or the *central self*. It is the responsible and rational, wise and mature part of the self. The central self observes the other parts of the self, the latter being more aggressive and adventurous. A leader needs to be self-reflective or mindful; we imagine the central self leading the way. The central self grows healthy and secure when born into relationships that are accepting, loving, and caring. When the central self is insecure or feels threatened, those feelings affect every aspect of one's being, as well as one's choices and actions, even as it fuels the inner critic and the exciting self, which we'll introduce. The central self engages mentors and beloved figures such as a favorite family member, professor, or mentor, but also forms of wisdom as well as life-giving activities. As our sensible self, the central self's work includes maintaining a close relationship with the other two parts of the self: *the inner critic* and the *exciting self*.

The *inner critic*, as the second part of the self, is the internalization of especially critical and punitive voices we heard and of uncaring relationships we had in childhood. These relationships—each one embodied by a person—frustrated and rejected us for what we needed and for who we are. We needed to be vulnerable and sought comfort, for example, but were called upon to "be strong" or worse; our needs were never recognized. Those voices now return as our voice—our inner critic. The inner critic persecutes, attacks, shames, and blames. It never affirms or supports or encourages. The critic is relentless in its pursuit. That Fairbairn also referred to this voice as the "internal saboteur" is an apt description as the voice sabotages our well-being.

We imagine you being at a meeting and wanting to contribute to the conversation. You were hesitant, however, wondering whether the contribution would be valued or perceived as coming out of the left field, dynamics linked to belonging and competence. A moment to speak arrives, but you hold back, and then the conversation goes somewhere else, leaving you and your contribution behind. Later, back in your office, your inner critic berates you for missing the perfect moment. Driving home, your inner critic continues its castigations for not having spoken earlier, giving you the very sentences you should have used while telling you the whole committee negatively judged your silence. Another time you may have been surprised by an event. The critic states you should have seen it coming. And, in an exceptionally busy period, the voice reminds you your parenting is inadequate, your children are suffering because of you. Due to problematic cultural expectations around motherhood, women in leadership often have a particularly loud inner critic telling them they can be better mothers.

The inner critic, whose creativity knows no bounds, completely ignores contexts, best practices followed, or the reality of time constraints. The punitive self-contempt the inner critic fuels undermines personal self-worth and professional confidence. The critic makes you feel like an imposter, one who does not belong, and it threatens that others will soon discover you to be the fraud you know you are.

As the inner critic drags us through the mud, it awakens the *exciting self,* which Fairbairn also called *the libidinal ego.* The exciting self seeks pleasure and craves excitement. It, too, is formed in early childhood and informed by playful, alluring, seductive, and even irresponsible relationships. Whereas the central self seeks relationships with wise, mature, even idealized persons, the exciting self, beginning in the teenage years, focuses only on parts of persons—often an external sex organ, a butt, or a breast—and turns a person into an object of desire or to be manipulated. The exciting self rarely notices the complexity within persons, relational dynamics, or situations. Without this self, the porn industry (but also the advertising world in general), which is so skilled at objectifying bodies, would be greatly diminished.

We need the exciting part for it gives us much joy and pleasure. Its sole task is to uplift our mood and excitement, especially after the inner critic sabotages our well-being. The dilemma we face, however, is that the exciting self never discerns, estimates, or evaluates—a task belonging to the central self. *The exciting self does not recognize or follow moral or ethical codes* and, as such, can bring havoc into a leader's life.

Fairbairn's tripartite view of the self provides us with a possible framework to understand what might have played out for Tiger Woods. He may very well disagree with this assessment, but we imagine him growing up in a military home, which placed high expectations on him, that discipline defined much of the parenting style he received, resulting in Woods having a very active inner critic. Though his outward appearance is most often of someone in complete control and Stoic in moments of personal discomfort, his internal dynamics are less tranquil. We imagine his inner critic berating him after a missed putt, a poorly executed shot, or a tournament "lost." Woods' inner critic, we imagine, reminds him he failed his father's expectations, not his own, of not only changing golf, but the whole world. With an aggressive inner critic, we can expect his exciting self jumping to come to his "rescue"—which of course was not a rescue at all. It's the exciting self's lack of discernment that got Woods in trouble.

Diagrammed, the three parts of your self show the self's inner dynamics (Figure 1.1).

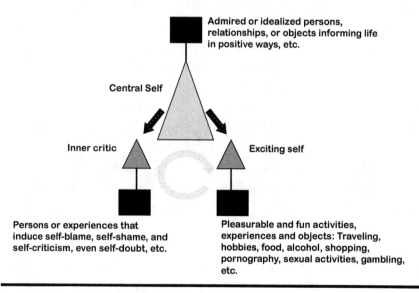

Figure 1.1   The tripartite self.

This diagram reflects the complexity of human nature. Any one of the three "selves" can drive you and your leadership. You have a rational side seeking what's best, wanting to be in control. It's the part of you that allows you to be a less anxious presence in times of crisis. It helps you keep healthy boundaries as you pursue your professional goals. When you are leading with excellence, this self is most visible to others. Your inner critic, however, reminds you of being a fraud about to be discovered. It scolds you for not being good enough to lead, that you are incompetent, or do not belong, that you have no control over what is happening, or that others are controlling you. Of course, this part of you is mostly hidden from others and plays out as an inner dialogue. When the inner critic is berating us, we often retreat in silence as if to lick our wounds, a retreat others can observe and find confusing. Soon the critic activates the exciting self, seeking to bring joy to our troubled self, but does so without any discernment, regardless of personal, professional, financial, or other costs.

How do you recognize the three parts within you? How can you best lead knowing you have three distinct parts? How will others recognize that you are leading from your central self?

Leaders really only have two basic choices: One option is empowering the central self to dialogue with both the inner critic and the exciting self (the two arrows next to the central self). The other option is abandoning themselves to an endless feedback loop between the inner critic dragging them down and the exciting self-creating excitement in thoughtless attempts at boosting a self-straining under the inner critic (See Figure 1.1). Like the circus artiste who stands on the backs of two horses, the audience expecting at every second the two horses will diverge leaving the rider either teetering on one horse or crashing to the ground, so too being mindful of the self's inner workings is crucial work. The performer's "crucial work" is to keep the reins taut, not allowing the horses to drift apart too far.

As one matures as a person and leader, the central self engages the inner critic in dialogue. So the next time your inner critic reminds you did a poor job, reply: "I did the best I could with the time and information I had" or something similar. When it provides the perfect comeback statement you could've given, you say: "Yes, I could have said that, but it would have shamed the other person and added fuel to the fire." When your inner critic calls you a poor parent, defend yourself by saying parenting requires many people, not just one, and you create and value quality time with your loved ones. In short, the more you challenge your inner critic—if possible even trying to determine whose voices and what experiences you internalized—the quieter it will get. As you live and lead from your central self, it can discern whether the inner critic has a point to prove or not. If you are not present as a parent, for example, change your ways and let your central self lead you in parenting. If you have made an error in judgment, prepare better next time and remain well-informed of trends, data, and research.

Likewise, when your exciting self tells you to seek the thrill of speed, arrange a track day where you can go as fast as you can without putting others at risk. If it suggests another drink, choose a non-alcoholic one or savor the one you have slowly over good conversation. Resist the exciting self's tendency to drink alone, drink with strangers, or take a drink to bed. Should the exciting self awaken a hunger in you and drive you to food, find a healthy snack or meal, or maybe you'll discover you are not hungry at all. Should the excitement manifest as shopping, rethink the benefits of same-day deliveries and the environmental cost of returning what was purchased without much discernment. If the exciting self takes you to gambling, remember the house always wins and place limits to protect your finances. As it hands you a joint to smoke during an interview, something we saw Elon Musk did, kindly decline.

There are many ways the central self can partner with the exciting self to instill joy and satisfaction with a keen awareness of limits, boundaries, and ethics.

You will falter as a leader if you hand over your leadership to either the inner critic or the exciting self. When leading from the inner critic, doubt and second-guessing will surround your leadership. You will cultivate a system of skeptics, always ready to criticize, doubt, blame, and even shame. Such leaders are easily recognized, for they cannot keep staff or stop projecting onto others. Conversely, if you hand your leadership to your exciting self, you are likely to fuel anxiety into your system, for the exciting part enjoys high energy and even chaos. Or worse, it will lead you to cross all kinds of boundaries, bringing disciplinary, ethical, and other charges against you. It can also put you and others physically at risk. The exciting self might try to rationalize your behavior, but the central selves of others will judge your actions and hold you accountable, making your excitement short-lived. With your exciting self, you might be able to stimulate some interest in a wild, exciting vision, but it too will be short-lived. After presenting your vision, the inner critic will tell you: "What were you thinking?" Lead from the central self; it is a wise choice.

Leading with wisdom is a choice

Leaders Show up as Whole Persons

You bring yourself to your leadership. Show up as a leader who instills confidence in others and as a facilitator of change. Often, the professional who was excelling in their profession and now assumes a leadership position has had minimal leadership training. It is much like parenting where we do not have in-depth training to become parents, other than a few Lamaze classes, yet we do become parents. Culture has warped values in this regard. Leadership experiences in college or university were circumscribed, occurred in safe spaces, and carried little risk but high reward. Professional education and formation give little or no attention to the selves we are. The ways we raise children and validate students, where everyone is a winner, undermine the formation of a whole and healthy self portraying authenticity, vulnerability, and an ability to sustain difficult conversations over time. The illusion is created that a strong cognitive-rational approach to life translates into being an effective leader.

If the insights of this book remain merely "interesting" with minimal emotional, relational, and professional implications, your life and leadership are likely to stay unchanged. Leadership must be cultivated, a task the educational system in especially the United States does poorly.

Dr. Smith, feeling overwhelmed as chair of his department and stuck in tension-filled relationships with increased expectations to deliver results, responded by following through with his personal goal to return to tennis—a sport he loves but had stopped playing due to lack of time. He invited department chairs to lunch, risked sharing how he was experiencing his tenure as chair, and asked for advice. To his surprise, he discovered that all the chairs felt somewhat overwhelmed, though they had never let on. He also asked to meet with the nursing director and office coordinator to learn more about the frustrations the nurses and admin staff had. Still facing a staff exodus, he decided to do hour-long exit interviews with those who resigned. At home, he apologized to his daughter for blaming her for empty liquor bottles. Sharing a love for music, they decided to work with a guitar teacher and covenanted to practice together one night a week. To his surprise, he needs less Scotch, and things are moving in positive directions, at work, and at home.

Prof. Ludouw also took strides in her leadership. She recognized her receiving fewer grants as a loss and is grieving the resulting changes. Invited by a friend, she started volunteering at a shelter for transient persons, where she found persons with early onset dementia wrestling a life from the streets. She revisited the reasons why she became a caregiver in the first place and discovered renewed satisfaction in working with people. She sought out a specialist assisting women in menopause and addressing hormonal imbalances, which greatly diminished her migraines. Her energy is rebounding and her intimate life has returned to being life-giving for her and her partner.

You are a complex person who leads and manages, among numerous personal and professional tasks. The illusion that one can lead in ways denying or defying one's self is powerful but remains an illusion. Looking carefully at who we are as leaders is a practice worth doing. In this chapter, we used two lenses to look at who we are as leaders. We said leaders bring a certain personality to our leadership, one we rely on every day to lead, but also one exposing our Achilles' heel. We also bring three "selves" demanding constant conversation with each other. When the inner critic and the exciting self dominate, we undermine our potential as leaders and get ourselves into personal, relational, professional, ethical, and even legal trouble. Next, we place ourselves in relational systems, for there is never just a leader, only a leader embedded in several intertwined systems, representing one's family; the workplace; the national and global situations; and the worlds of finance, culture, and even nature. Family systems theory is a crucial lens through which to view leadership.

Notes

1. John Macmurray, *The Self as Agent* (London: Faber & Faber, 1957), 101. Emphasis original.
2. Kimberly P. Brown,Richard J. Iannelli, and Danielle P. Marganoff, "Use of the Personality Assessment Inventory in Fitness-for-Duty Evaluations of Physicians," *Journal of Personality Assessment* 99, no. 5 (2017).
3. Larry Harmon, and Raymond Pomm, "Evaluation, Treatment, and Monitoring of Disruptive Physician Behavior," *Psychiatric Annals* 34, no. 10 (2004).
4. Jessica H. Stacy,"Impaired Physicians and the MMPI-2: Comparison and Profiles by Impairment Type" (PhD. Dissertation, University of San Diego, 2017).
5. W. Ronald D. Fairbairn, Endopsychic Structure Considered in Terms of Object-Relationships in *Psychoanalytic Studies of the Personality* (New York: Routledge, 1996).

Chapter 2

Engaging Emotional Systems: Understanding the Anxiety within Change

To lead is to know one's place and function in a larger system and to discern the system's emotional process. The process reflects the relational and behavioral patterns created by all who make up a system. Leaders thus find themselves in many systems—personal, familial, educational, cultural, professional, corporate, financial, also ecclesial and political—which are all intricately linked. The belief of leading unaffected by or disconnected from the emotional processes around us or disconnected from others is false. It also assures less effective leadership.

Identifying a person intertwined with systems became a focus in the 1950s when psychiatrist Murray Bowen spearheaded what became known as Family Systems Theory, though ancient Egyptian and Mayan cultures already drew on similar insights. Rabbi Edwin Friedman, who worked closely

DOI: 10.4324/9781003463993-4

with Bowen, expanded the wisdom of systems theory to
leadership. Though every leader is part of several systems,
one system is unique to every leader: the system their family
of origin created. Leaders who lack self-awareness and insight
into how that early formation shaped them are likely to repeat
in their leadership the dynamics they first experienced in
childhood and with family members. In our families of origin, we first learned how to relate, how to manage anxiety,
how to respond to exits—deaths, moves, and divorces—and
entrances—births, arriving in a new town, and new relationships—and how to survive moments of danger, tension,
and crisis. No person escapes the anxiety of the system that
birthed them alongside many overlapping systems. Anxiety or
tension, which we use interchangeably, is the natural reaction
to a perceived or real threat or the way the members of the
system do life together, i.e., change. Repeating old patterns of
behavior facing anxiety rarely serve leadership well.

Evonne Taylor feels stuck. Management charged her with
improving morale after the company was forced to lay off staff
in a period of financial downturn. As producers of high-end
pet food, their system was not sufficiently open to change
as pet owners became more discerning about where they
will spend their money. Management called upon Evonne
as she is well-loved by her co-workers and a proven leader.
Although everyone would agree that the company morale is
low, Evonne assembled a team around her to poll the level
of morale among employees and to discern specific pressure
points beyond the layoffs. The team had a good idea of what
the issues are, but sought to be transparent in their approach.

Evonne's team received strong pushback when the survey
was announced. Members of the senior management questioned its need, stating morale is not as low as people report
and employees should have more resilience to the challenges
the company is facing. Their company, after all, is in the same
boat as many other companies. Evonne was reminded that

prior financial downturns were worse than the current one and the company prevailed in those times. Evonne noticed most of these voices were coming from white, male leaders in the last season of their professional careers. She decided not to confront these voices, believing the survey will back her and her team. Other employees told Evonne and her team morale is worse than any survey will indicate, for employees have no trust in the system. They cannot be honest in their feedback for fear of retribution. This group too felt any survey would be a waste of time. Another group of employees expressed gratitude to Evonne and her team, saying their work will save the company from further layoffs. They had no feedback or recommendations to offer but restated their belief in Evonne. A fourth group surfaced among the employees. This group used a closed online forum to bemoan how low the morale is and discussed all things wrong in the company. Evonne and her team were excluded from this forum, but hardly a day went by without someone sharing some of the online activity with Evonne. They would wonder out loud how Evonne is going to respond to the closed forum's growing membership.

As the pressure around Evonne's team increased, they disagreed on how best to proceed. To her surprise, members of her team began to echo the voices she heard from administration and staff. Evonne tried to bridge the differences, even increasing the times her team met, but made little headway. She used some vacation time to create a survey and decided not to share her work with her team, for they would disagree on the content. Unable to reach common ground and frustrated by Evonne bypassing them, some of her team resigned in protest. Evonne, who fully expected her charge to be difficult but also felt equipped to rise to the occasion, suddenly started doubting her competency.

Evonne feels stuck. No surprise. She is in a difficult position from which bringing change is near impossible. Her senior colleagues are downplaying the staff's concerns as well as the charge they gave her. They blame employees for a lack of backbone. Fellow employees argue that the low morale is just the tip of the iceberg, a mere symptom of something much deeper and sinister in an untrustworthy system. Others have unrealistic expectations about what Evonne and her team can accomplish. The "silent," disgruntled online group particularly concerns Evonne as they exhibit passive-aggressive behavior and refuse to be part of any solution.

As Evonne's team struggles to settle into its charge, it becomes clear to Evonne that her team is reflecting dysfunction in the company that predates her arrival. Moreover, the same dynamics can be identified in the family of the couple who founded the company. She is responding to the stress around her by taking on more responsibilities, including tasks she previously delegated to her team. Even though she does not appreciate others micromanaging her, she now finds herself slipping into a way of leading she would typically question.

As Evonne drove home after another stress-filled day, questions flooded her mind: *How can she help her senior colleagues see the situation more clearly? How can she reach out to the group not trusting her as a proxy for the company's management and board? How can she communicate realistic expectations, given how challenging it is to address staff morale in the company and continued financial insecurities? Might there be ways to invite the employees who are passive-aggressive to partake in a town hall or other kind of meeting? Would such a meeting even work? How can she increase transparency in the system? What will people think of her if she is unable to address morale and more layoffs follow?* And then she wonders: *Did the mostly male leadership set her up to fail so a woman can be blamed?* Her inner critic berates her, telling her she could have intervened some time ago. Becoming angry with herself, she wonders how she can reclaim a leadership style affirming others and stop her micromanaging.

What Evonne is not realizing is her dance at work is one she danced before in her family of origin. Her father, an immigrant to the United States, was an unemotional man who believed people can pick themselves up by their bootstraps, just as he did. He never affirmed Evonne throughout her stellar academic career, always communicating he expects more of her, that her primary task is to secure a financial future for herself. Though he was never abusive, he was a "hard" man. Her mother suffered greatly under her dad's distant and rational worldview. Mom would never counter dad, always reminding the three children that their dad is older and wiser than they are, had given up much so they could have something, and should be respected. Evonne's younger sister rebelled against her dad and caused much tension in the family. Her father would say her sister is humiliating the family and is a disappointment. That Evonne's sister left university to become a recognized artist does not seem to impress their father. Many times Evonne would clean up the messes her sister made—literally and figuratively—in order to keep her father's wrath at bay. The sleepovers her sister arranged during their teenage years were the worst, as they left the house in chaos. Evonne and her mom would clean the house before everyone woke up. In recent years, she has helped her sister overcome a few financial situations. Her brother, however, was born when the sisters were already in primary school and could get away with murder. He received a different set of rules, was rarely disciplined, but received praise for poor performance. He managed to move under his parents' radar. Evonne does not have a strong relationship with her brother. They only call each other on birthdays. She knows little about his life and he does not know much about hers, including her frustration with their sister who can make rash decisions. Evonne is slowly discovering that the dance of leadership most often follows the steps first danced in one's family of origin. Systems always repeat themselves.

Systems always repeat themselves, for good or ill

Leaders who recognize there are systemic forces affecting their leadership are less likely to get caught up in relational dynamics frustrating change and growth. As we authors consult with institutions and companies, we find leaders who believe leadership is either a cognitive-rational exercise or an exercise of charisma and power over others. These leaders look at a situation, collect data, consult with others, make a rational decision, empower, and equip folk with the skills needed, and wait for employees to implement the decisions made and visions given. One would think such an approach should work—but it rarely does. "Perhaps data collection serves as a way of avoiding the emotional variables," writes Friedman in his *A Failure of Nerve: Leadership in the Age of the Quick Fix*.[1]

A curious leader will discover many benefits from incorporating systems theory into a personal philosophy and the practice of leadership. Here, we highlight five core, interrelated systemic principles that can guide one's leadership: recognizing the emotional process, identifying intertwined systems, self-differentiating from the system managing systemic reactions, and overcoming a system's resistance to change.

The emotional process drives relationships and the choices we make

The Emotional Process—The Power of an Invisible Force

On our evolutionary journey, before our cognitive abilities evolved, we were emotional creatures who simply tried to survive. Sense perception was and remains the primary protection against danger. As a result of this evolution, we have two ways in which we approach the world: one emotional and the other rational. As Bowen reminds us:

> The emotional system is a naturally occurring system in all forms of life that enables an organism to receive information from within itself and from the environment [and] to integrate that information and respond on the basis of it. The emotional system includes mechanisms such as those involved in finding and obtaining food, reproducing, fleeing enemies, rearing young, and other aspects of social relationships. It includes responses that range from the most automatic instinctual ones to those that contain a mix of automatic and learned elements.[2]

Whether individual or systemic, the *emotional process* is a natural, highly reactionary response and may be seen as rather basic, resisting change, but not unchangeable. The emotional process is functional in nature; it seeks to minimize anxiety. It operates at the unconscious level unless one works hard to bring it to awareness. Also, the emotional process changes according to the situation. The *intellectual system*, in turn, gives us the ability to think and reflect, and enables a person to govern life through logic, intellect, and reason. Whereas the intellectual system appreciates data (information) and deliberate discernment, the emotional system will discern in a split second whether a situation is dangerous or not, readying a person to remain calm, fight, or flee.

The emotional process sees a person as a complex being that evolved from simple forms of life yet remains instinctively linked to all living things. Intellectual functioning may distinguish us from much in the natural world, but it does not remove our deep connection to all things living. The feeling system assures human survival. It defines instinct, reproduction, the autonomic nervous system, and one's subjective emotional states. A human is thus an emotional being first before any intellectual functioning takes place.

How one feels—experiences emotion—and thinks—rationally discerns—is foundational to systems theory. The degree to which a person distinguishes the feeling process from the thinking process distinguishes one person from another. Typically, followers do not discern the feeling and thinking processes tying them to a leader. Such relationships occur mostly as an unconscious reactivity. How much emotional fusion one can find between a person and their system(s) is discernible and can be used not only as a predictor of a pattern of living, but also to reflect the level of health in the system. Enmeshed systems where there is little differentiation between different members, especially around diverse thought, reflect systems that become dangerous, even cultic. Cults do survive, but usually not for very long and without leaving a legacy of destruction.

Leaders fail at initiating change when they underestimate the power of the emotional foundations of our personal lives and the institutions we build, whether it is our intimate relationships and families, our institutions or corporations, or our societies and nations. These leaders have not reckoned with emotional processes resisting, deflecting, denying, or speeding up decisions, interactions, and behavior to such a degree that the desired change buckles under its weight or derails in a speed wobble. When leaders seek the "right" member for their team or institution, they forget the primary question: *What is happening in the system for any fit to be there for this person? Who is this person who needs to manage the emotional process of which we are a part? What kind of leader does the emotional process need to assure transformation?* A prospective employee with a wonderful résumé, who has risen above others due to their cognitive-rational acumen, may very well be someone stuck in emotional systems, always becoming reactive or immobilized to moments of tension. They might not be the "right" colleague or employee after all.

Emotional processes come before and outlast any leader

The emotional process can be recognized in a system's:

- Relational patterns—who agrees, who stirs conflict, who resists, who distances, who derails a process—indicating reactions to anxiety in a system.
- Communication skills within the system and between its members: whose voices are heard and who remain a silent presence.
- Power and authority lines: who has responsibility with little authority, and who has authority with little responsibility.
- Decision-making processes: how reactivity, collaboration, transparency, engaging conflicting truths, and secrecy affect discernment; who and what are excluded from discernment.
- Ability to manage conflict and sustain difficult conversations: this includes bringing in marginalized voices.
- Ability to create a place of interdependent belonging: who is part of the system or wants to belong to the system, who is or wants out, and who will never be invited in or pushed out. And,
- The emotional process discloses how the system engages other systems, whether internal, local, national, or international.

The emotional process of a system is difficult to define due to its abstract nature, yet manifests in specific, recognizable ways.

Its effects are clear. *The emotional process can be seen* as *the energy flowing through a system determining not only relationships, but also how people think about their here-and-now, discern their futures, act, and engage in change.* Though the emotional system presents itself in varied ways, it is a single emotional process with diverse interrelated parts. Any one of the parts can derail the whole process. Murray Bowen referred to the emotional process as the *undifferentiated* (meaning pervasive and poorly defined) *family ego mass,* which includes one's extended family.[3] Unresolved issues in any person or part of the system can determine the dance all are dancing. A leader whose personal life leaves them tension-filled brings tension into their workplace; a supervisor who avoids personal conflict will avoid disagreements; a team member who resists change can derail any process, regardless of their position in the corporate hierarchy.

> The emotional process determines all relationships and behavior

Since the emotional process reigns supreme, understanding and finding ways to differentiate oneself from that process—containing one's emotional reactivity while using one's cognitive capacities—are central to one's leadership. Knowing how the emotional process manifests in its intertwined ways can help you become an expert at facilitating change.

Identifying Intertwined Systems—Why Linear Thinking Fails

A certain pitfall in leadership is believing in linear—cause-and-effect—thinking (Figure 2.1). This kind of thinking suggests that to get to Goal E, all one has to do is go through Steps A, B, C, and D and at which point Goal E will unfold.

Figure 2.1 Linear thinking.

Linear thinking implicates the leader who thinks charging a team with a task will lead to change. It is the leader who does not supervise effectively, most often to avoid supervision's inherent moments of tension and intimacy, and who does not empower others to succeed. We imagine this leader passing their responsibility to bring change to a junior member in the system, typically someone who has less institutional authority. Should this junior leader—who has aspirations of becoming a senior leader—follow their supervisor's example, they will, in turn, pass their newly received responsibility to others with even less authority to bring change. Even if the junior leader is competent, their work will still be compromised as their supervisor, who is part of the emotional process, is not functioning at an optimal level. Certainly, not all charged with tasks have the competence or experience, or authority to facilitate a change process. As responsibility is passed from one person to another, the ball can be dropped anywhere along the hierarchy.

In linear thinking, there are definite first and second steps, followed by additional steps, with Goals A to E not only independent of each other but also independent of the system of which they are a part. The independent nature of these goals fuels a few illusions:

The first illusion is that one can plug any truth or new data into a system and it will effectively bring transformation to the system. "How to" books rely on this illusion. They tell their readers what to do and, irrespective of one's system, expect results. Diets, typically leaving systems and emotional processes untouched, rely on this principle too, with an estimated 95% of diets failing.

The second illusion is assuming a result has an identifiable "cause" or source. The belief is clear: Change the problematic cause and the problem will disappear. Cause-and-effect thinking does not recognize the intertwined nature of the systems of which we are a part. Dr. Smith's clinic, as we wrote earlier, has many members, from patients to nurses, doctors, administrators, and custodians, who all need to function optimally to make the clinic efficient. No single stakeholder can bring effective change should member stakeholders resist change.

Emotional systems, as with change, are complex processes

The third illusion, implicated in the previous two, is the illusion of simplicity. Cause-and-effect thinking provides "easy," even clear and undisputable solutions. Your institution, however, is a complex system containing many interrelated mini-systems (as Evonne discovered about her company) while it engages larger systems on the national and international stages. Excellent leaders recognize that intertwined mini-systems collectively form the larger system. Such leaders can engage the system from any point and resist any linear notion of cause-and-effect leadership. The more complex the system is perceived, the higher the possibility of effective transformation.

A leader who embraces the emotional process in their organization recognizes the intertwined nature of an emotional process (Figure 2.2). As they imagine Goals A to E, they see:

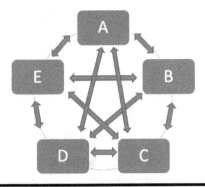

Figure 2.2   The web of relationships in systems.

Since A, B, C, and D are interwoven and interdependent, they all influence E, even as the different variables can individually be identified. Each component operates as part of a larger whole. The groups Evonne encountered—from the aloof and judgmental executives to the passive-aggressive and skeptical online forum—together form the system. Addressing just one group or coming up with a one-size-fits-all plan will lead her nowhere, as the components do not function according to their *nature* but according to their *position* in the network. *The position implies a certain role and function, and these rarely stay the same because the system is always in flux.* Evonne's executives communicate the situation is not as bad as the staff think, including the staff who lost their jobs; others are saying things are worse than most think. Should she be successful in finding a way to increase morale, the executives may begin to communicate the new morale does not show sufficient trust in the leaders, whereas others may not be troubled by morale anymore, but rather the poor financial situation of the company, blaming the leaders for financial mismanagement. The system will be in the same tension-filled position Evonne received when she was charged, with only the issues shifting. Being mindful of a person or group's position in a system highlights the importance of how the various parts of the system relate to one another.

> In an emotional process, roles and functions are primary

For leaders, the gift of intertwined systems is fourfold: First, one can get to Goal E by starting anywhere in the system. Like a spider's web, the system will react to any change, regardless of where in the system change is introduced. This is important for leaders, for if you seek to change your institution, changing the way you lead can be the most effective way to get there. Wise leaders facilitate change by changing themselves before they seek change in others, their team, or institution. Second, intertwined systems remove the tendency to focus on whatever is perceived to be "the problem." Something such as low morale (Evonne's problem) is only a *symptom* of deeper and possibly more dangerous concerns, such as a leadership out of touch with those they lead or a system that has lost its agility in the pet food market. A third benefit of intertwined systems is one can bring change by *adding* to the system or by beginning something new. *Adding* new behavior—increased transparency around how decisions are made or more opportunities to provide feedback to leadership or investing in the formation of employees, for example—is more effective at initiating change than *stopping* behavior or *removing* problems. Thus, announcing a rule that private forums or chat rooms will not be tolerated, will not work or curb the problem. By adding to the system, weekly town hall meetings, for example, the problem area can be isolated to such an extent the symptom may very well disappear. And fourth, the intertwined nature of systemic membership removes the privilege of hierarchy or separation between leaders and followers. Leaders and followers are part of one unit, one needs the other to thrive.

The difference between linear thinking and discernment that considers the intertwined nature of systems can further be highlighted through *first*-order and *second*-order change.

First- and Second-order Change

Family systems theory distinguishes between first- and second-order change. First-order change offers a simple solution to a problem, leaving the wider system unchanged. Second-order change inherently transforms the system. Whereas first-order change takes relatively little "work," second-order change takes intention, time, and effort. Imagine a room that is too hot in summer and too cool in winter. The first-order change would be bringing in a more powerful HVAC system to cool the room in summer and heat it in winter. Second-order change might be discovering that the insulation in the room is insufficient, the windows let in much outside air or let air escape, and the basement's crawlspace has no insulation. Addressing the concern now implies bringing in insulation and replacing the old windows with new triple-paned windows. The existing HVAC unit is suddenly sufficient. Whereas first-order change leaves the system unchanged, second-order change changes the system itself.

Second-order change changes the system

One hospital system sought ways to diminish burnout among physicians and increase physician retention. The first-order change included longer daycare hours, additional parking possibilities, placing more printers in units, offering better dining choices, and new policies around paid time off. Although appreciated by physicians, the larger system remained largely untouched by these changes, easily recognized in the little "cost" to the system other than some initial financial output.

Seeking second-order change, the leadership added "Wellness" as a core value to the institution's mission statement. With "Wellness" as the central focus—not burnout or retention or another problem—things began to shift. Supervisors, for example, are now being evaluated on the wellness of their teams and are tasked with retaining their staff. Furthermore, wellness is recognized in every part of the system; though wellness for physicians is different from the wellness of nurses or the wellness of the laboratory staff or other employees, the system as a whole relies on everyone to assure optimal functioning and reach its goals and mission.

The hospital soon recognized that first-order change is much easier to accomplish than second-order change. For this institution, second-order change is constantly being resisted and undermined. Competent leaders can facilitate second-order change. They also manage reactivity within the emotional process.

Managing Systemic Reactivity

When a system becomes anxious, often in reaction to a threat, which includes perceived change, a leader can expect certain responses from the system's emotional process. First, some members of the community will seek emotional *distance*, even to the point of physically leaving the system. Those who distance themselves will not respond to emails or will have delayed responses. They will not speak their mind in meetings and they will pull away from core relationships. Second, other members will react to anxiety by seeking *enmeshment*. This is a deceptive emotional closeness and a groupthink in which the members feel alike, act alike, and hope alike. Feeling threatened by those who think, act, and hope differently, this group speaks with one voice. Third, others yet will gossip, keep secrets, create moments of pseudo-intimacy, and engage in a dynamic called *triangulation*. The latter principle speaks to two persons or groups—let's call them A and B—in tension or conflict and unable to resolve the tension. A and B then rope in a third entity—C—with whom the grievances are shared and who now lives with the tension (see Figure 7.1). Parents know triangulation intimately from their child playing the two parents off against each other. Triangulation, like other emotional reactions, is an unconscious act. The more triangles in a system, the more stuck the system is. Leaders are often triangulated into relationships since people rightly believe they can make a difference. There are other responses too when an emotional process is filled with anxiety.

Fourth, some in the system will become hostile and *conflict* will increase, often around issues or concerns on the periphery of the system. Suddenly Evonne's team disagreed to such an extent that some members left the team. Conflict inspires bullies to pursue others, for bullies silently believe "What is happening is your fault as a leader. It is my task to remind you of your failure."

A fifth and final response within the system facing anxiety is for those members who *overfunction*, i.e., literally seeking ways to function *for* you as a leader, even to the point of taking over your leadership responsibilities (because they silently believe you are not sufficiently competent to lead them in this situation). An unaware junior leader easily overfunctions toward a senior leader. Others will notice and resist the junior leader's leadership. The overfunctioner's unconscious communication is: "You need my help. You are struggling and I can fix you or the situation. No need to ask, but here I am" Other members, in turn, will *underfunction*, unconsciously handing over their responsibilities—for productivity, excellence, etc. to others on the team or to you as leader. The underfunctioner communicates: "Others are doing much better than I am and I'll never be like them. Poor me." Of course, you as a leader or team can overfunction too, taking on others' responsibilities, setting goals lacking mutuality, and treating those you lead as if they cannot function without you. Do this and those you lead may not even be able to recall the mutual goals toward which you are working. Inevitably, every overfunctioner underfunctions in various aspects of their personal and professional lives, neglecting personal and professional goals, rarely asking for advice, and finding themselves stuck in relationships of distance, enmeshment, and conflict.

In a leadership class that draws on play theory, Jaco teaches his students how to juggle. Juggling can be a metaphor for effective leadership. One year, the class included a student whose childhood injury prevented them from juggling with both hands. Despite being invited to forego this exercise, the student opted in. Every ball they threw into the air dropped on the ground. They repeated this exercise without success or despair. Other students stopped their juggling practice to pick up the balls the student dropped. The student never asked their peers to do so. A number of the students in the seminar angrily blamed Jaco for being insensitive and "forcing" the student to partake. When Jaco told the students partaking was their peer's choice, they would not believe him. Overfunctioners easily assume the responsibilities of others. The student, in turn, allowed the students to continue picking up the dropped balls, underfunctioning toward his action. Those who picked up the dropped balls not only interrupted their personal practice, they assured the student with the injury could continue in a fixed pattern, having delegated some responsibility to them.

Moses, the Jewish leader we mentioned, was a recognized underfunctioner. Having led his people in circles in the desert, we read, he did manage to procure manna and quail as food, and saw a rock becoming a fountain with flowing water—miracles ascribed to God. He was a sought-after source of wisdom and people lined up from early to late for Moses to judge the various situations in their lives.[4] While he was preoccupied with his people, he sent his wife and sons back to his father-in-law, Jethro, a taboo in Moses' time. Moses neglected his responsibilities as a partner and a parent as he claimed to be a leader. Jethro, fed up with this situation, returned his daughter and Moses' wife, Zipporah, to Moses. Seeing people in long lines waiting for Moses, Jethro challenged Moses' leadership. Becoming defensive in the face of this challenge, Moses' narcissism shone through: "The people come to me … I decide," he said. Between a few more "me's" and "I's," Moses tells us he is the indispensable one and his community would struggle without his wisdom. Jethro then mentored Moses: "What you are doing is not good. You and these people who come to you will only wear yourselves out." Jethro suggested Moses empower other leaders to take most cases, leaving only the more difficult situations for him to address. Moses listened to his father-in-law and created a corporate style of management in which the work was divided among teams of people Moses supervised. Moses identified small teams of tens, with leaders supervising groups of fifties, hundreds, and even thousands. In Moses, we have a leader who curbed his overfunctioning/underfunctioning nature.

A leader who overfunctions carries much anxiety and is easily frustrated or disappointed. They also underfunction towards their personal and professional lives. Since overfunctioning and underfunctioning are two ways of managing anxiety, any person assuming these roles indicates a threat to the emotional process. Evonne, one can say, was a "perfect" choice for her superiors. They were not responsive to what was going on for some time—thus underfunctioning as leaders—whereas Evonne's family taught her all about assuming responsibility for others—overfunctioning.

Anxious systems have parts distancing, enmeshing, triangulating, entering conflict, while underfunctioning and overfunctioning

Leadership Tasks in the Face of Systemic Anxiety

Since a leader can expect anxious reactivity in any system when a threat appears or as change sets in, one's leadership tasks are clearly defined:

- *Bridge to persons who want to pull away from the conversation and process toward change.* Invite the silent voices to share. Resist pursuing folk who want to leave, but engage them around their frustrations with a curious and compassionate ear.
- *Bring distance between yourself and those seeking to form an uncritical union with you.* Resist enmeshment. Share your fears and even incompetencies with this group as such vulnerability will disabuse them that you are a savior or that you all are like-minded.
- *Avoid triangles formed when you are pulled in by two persons in conflict or two opposing parties to judge who is right and who is wrong, or when*

you are called in to broker peace. Be confidential. Avoid gossip, for it triangulates all involved. The tension between those in conflict will be passed to you should you become the third person in a triangle. Imagine a toxic ball of anxiety thrown at you, which you reactively and instinctively catch. Holding on to the ball, however, also implies the toxins are entering your body. Pass the ball back as fast as possible. Empower the two persons and parties involved to resolve their tension. Widen the conversation by bringing in more conversation partners. Exit any dysfunctional triangles in which you find yourself in your personal life or family of origin—with parents, siblings, in-laws, between you and your partner, or with a child, even a social institution. Remember, systems repeat themselves for good and ill. We'll return to triangulation in Chapter Seven.

■ *Remain present in moments of conflict and discover the forces or dynamics behind the tension or conflict.* Reflect on *the way it is*—what is happening now—when the urge to envision the *way it should be*—hopes or a vision for the future—becomes strong (see the case of the Armonds in Chapter 7). Distinguish conflicts from disagreements. Disagreements are to be expected as many divergent ideas are entertained. Conflict, however, reflects a stuck system where there are only winners and losers. Remind yourself conflict is a symptom of the system telling you the emotional process is anxious and not functioning optimally.

■ *Function for yourself.* Be clear about your personal and professional goals and pursue those goals with purpose. Resist doing the emotional, relational, spiritual, and even financial work for others. Though overfunctioning will initially lower your anxiety, inevitably it leaves you and the other person or the system in a stuck position. Overfunctioning inevitably leads to burn-out. Your goal is neither to overfunction nor to underfunction, personally or professionally. You need to be differentiated—part of, yet separate from the system's unconscious responses— which we'll discuss in the next chapter.

Effective leaders are not consumed by the emotional process

Our intellectual system can convince us that managing systemic reactivity is a simple, easy-to-do part of leadership. Don't be fooled. The emotional system functions primarily at the instinctual level and the responses to anxiety in a system are rarely conscious choices. This anticipates members of a leadership team or employees "naturally" drifting toward enmeshment or distance, they suddenly find themselves in triangles of conflict, and they overfunction and underfunction without knowing they are doing so or choosing to do so. Persons and groups react to the increased stress according to the level of their self-differentiation, something they bring with them to their employment.

Without the ability to manage systemic reactions effectively, leaders will remain stuck in muddy waters or spiral alongside their system into chaos. Managing reactivity thus demands mindfulness of who you are as a leader. It requires quieting your inner critic and resisting reckless actions (see Chapter 1).

The work of self-differentiation (Chapter 3) and engaging the system becomes easier when you recognize that you can only bring yourself to your leadership and function for yourself.

The individual and systemic reactions also indicate a resistance to change.

Seeking and Resisting Change

Change is a constant due to internal and external forces affecting a system's emotional process. Yet, the system resists change and repeats itself. This dynamic of resisting change is called the *homeostatic principle* or the effort to maintain a system's *equilibrium*. Friedman defines homeostasis as "the tendency of any set of relationships to strive perpetually, in self-correcting ways, to preserve the organizing principles of its existence."[5] Homeostasis suggests a balance point with which the system is comfortable, a self-correcting dynamic protecting the system from additional anxiety or destruction. The dynamics of distancing, enmeshment, triangulation, overfunctioning, and conflict we mentioned are all systemic attempts to maintain homeostasis and thwart change.

Family therapists describe "the identified patient"—as the person in the system who takes on the anxiety in the system and becomes dysfunctional—giving the system the illusion that it is healthy. Imagine a couple experiencing unresolved conflict whose child is suddenly caught shoplifting or unexpectedly gets poor grades at school, bringing attention, systems of care, and accountability—all currently lacking in the parental relationship—to the family system. Here, the child became triangulated between the parents, and their tension now manifests in the child. The identified patient may be a person who presents with general poor performance, addictions, financial mismanagement, or even unethical acts. In institutions, the identified patient can be a team or group which suddenly underperforms to such an extent the whole system is at peril. Suddenly, all attention is given to this one part of the institution, leaving the rest of the institution untouched as the illusion is created that the troubling/troubled unit is independent of the wider system. As all the attention is now focused on a small part of the system, the homeostatic balance is protected. Even if the problems in this one team or group are fixed, the emotional process in the institution will remain unchanged, and soon another team or group will become the focus of attention as it manifests the dysfunction in the system's emotional process.

Whenever someone leaves a system or when someone joins a system—entrances and exits—the homeostasis is immediately altered. So too, when new processes and protocols are implemented or when someone communicates "difference" within the system. The difference may be a leader who seeks to break the hierarchical leadership style of an institution to be more collaborative or relational or transparent. It might be the leader who is authentic and self-differentiated, balancing thinking and feeling in a system, preferring overfunctioners that feel or think in compliance with the system's needs. The differentiated or "different" leader might also be the one who names the secrets the system is keeping. Differentiation always ignites systemic reactivity.

One company hired a consultant to help discern where the system's performance was breaking down. After being hired and after actively learning about the system, middle management wanted to review the consultant's résumé to validate their expertise. Middle management did not want the consultant to discover what was happening in and through their leadership. As the consultant immersed herself in various units in the institution, the institutional anxiety increased. *What is she doing here? What will she find? What will she report about us? To whom will she report it?* Middle management, who were informed by their supervisors that a consultant had been hired, "forgot" the consultant had already been hired and reports to their supervisors. They seemed unaware of the ways they were reacting to a new person joining the system.

Bowen writes when a system's equilibrium is upset, an "emotional shock wave" ripples through the system, potentially causing systemic reactivity that can last months or even years after the initial shock wave occurred.[6] Current events you face as a leader may be the result of decisions made by a predecessor or even by other systems your institution engages. In an ideal world, the previous leader would have handed over to you a well-functioning system and your system would be independent of other (unstable or dysfunctional) systems. Of course, this ideal world does not exist.

We cannot imagine a leader who is not tasked to upset the homeostasis of their system. *Who hires leaders with the expectation that they will maintain the status quo? What system is immune to people leaving or being added to the system?* Homeostasis demands that a leader has strategies to engage the systemic reactions one can expect when change occurs, as it always will. Effective leadership requires engaging the homeostatic principle alongside the diverse range of systemic reactions we've identified. No quick fix will save the day.

Overcoming Systemic Resistance to Change

Leaders who are driven by the perceived security of big data may find the call to pay attention to the emotional processes of one's personal and familial lives, and within a team or institution, tone-deaf. Trying to convince someone of the power of the system's emotional process is futile as the fable of the dead man in the Introduction teaches.

It takes courage and imagination to recognize and engage emotional processes and the reciprocal relationships determining much of our lives. When we choose to overlook or deny the importance of these forces and have observational myopia, we diminish the potential to lead visionary, sustained, and lasting transformation. Systems theory provides a proven, needed frame of reference for you as a leader. It empowers you to be responsive, responsible, ethical, committed, and less anxious than others in the system. It beckons clear thinking and communication, a maturity attractive to others. Of course, as leaders, we do engage data and make hard decisions to facilitate change, as well as explore possible scenarios, but emotion remains foundational to an institution's health.

As a leader, you need to be differentiated. A concept we'll explore next.

Notes

1. Friedman, *A Failure of Nerve: Leadership in the Age of the Quick Fix*, 27.
2. Murray Bowen and Michael E. Kerr, *Family Evaluation* (New York: W. W. Norton, 1988), 278.
3. Murray Bowen, *Family Therapy in Clinical Practice* (New York: J. Aronson, 1978), 113.
4. This narrative can be found in *The Bible*, Exodus 18.
5. Edwin H. Friedman, *Generation to Generation: Family Process in Church and Synagogue, Guilford Family Therapy Series* (New York: Guilford Press, 1985), 23.
6. Bowen, 325.

LEADING IN SYSTEMS

Chapter 3

Becoming Self-differentiated: Leading with Less Anxiety

"I feel like a small boy." These were the first words a newly appointed president of an academic institution uttered to his community. With deep emotion written all over his body and wiping away tears, he continued to recite, from memory, the lengthy speech of a relatively unknown Greek philosopher. His recitation was no surprise as he was renowned for his memory skills. After the quote, he briefly thanked the board chair for the trust placed in him and promised to serve the community with diligence. A couple of weeks later no one could recall anything else the president stated that day.

The president's tenure started under a dark cloud that made his words of serving his community come across as being disingenuous, if not hypocritical. Prior to being nominated as president, he was a colleague but for a variety of reasons he was not the choice of the community he was to lead. He lacked academic credentials, was a people pleaser, and was known to engage in culture wars. After he joined the

DOI: 10.4324/9781003463993-6

faculty years earlier, he aggrandized himself to the Board of Trustees, stepping into a void created by the departing president's poor functioning. When several senior faculty members raised concerns about their colleague's candidacy, the Board cut the search process short, broke protocol by not having the community interview the candidate, and announced their president.

Within weeks, the president used financial reasoning to fire core faculty with whom he had a conflictual relationship, even as a building project was announced. Some sued the institution and walked away with significant severance packages. He raised much money, but the money came from persons whose values were not reflected in the very community he led. Unable to be a buffer between his faculty, students, and core donors, some faculty left. When a long-serving faculty member wrote a book challenging traditional knowledge, the donors and conservative stakeholders demanded the faculty member be fired. Though the president could not do so due to tenure practices and academic freedom, he also did not protect the faculty member from attack; the latter aging considerably in little time. Beholden to his donors, the president changed the institution along narrow ideological lines, hiring faculty who supported his worldview. Students who found themselves at the margins of society became even more marginalized. One student committed suicide and implicated the institution's complicity in creating a culture fueling shame and self-hate. The president remained eerily absent as the community grieved the student's death, but reminded all that the student had mental health concerns. The school became marginalized amongst peer institutions.

The president had depressive tendencies, which he self-medicated with alcohol, a habit known to many. He kept impressing new audiences with his memory skills, but those who experienced him a second time wondered who the person was who only used the words of others. Was there an authentic person behind the persona created over the years?

The president sought retirement after a diagnosis of a neurological disease that robbed him of his memory. He left the institution in a precarious financial place as the conservative donors refused to embrace his successor.

A leader who does not function as a whole person and who cannot engage in the emotional processes of a system is destined to fail and bring about questionable change. *Who would become a leader knowing that the search process was interrupted due to tension amongst stakeholders, without doing much work to bridge to all and earn trust? Why did the board interrupt the search process when their preferred candidate became controversial? What does this case reveal about the emotional process of the Board and institution? Why could the president not discern the sources of his financial support? What insecurities did the president hide by memorizing texts and using the words of others? What is the responsibility of a system toward those directly and negatively impacted by the system's poor functioning? And what is the long-term future of this institution? Should you be asked to be a consultant to this institution, where would you begin to facilitate change? How might you address the obvious concerns of board functioning, leadership perceptions, engaging stakeholders and donors, and lack of trust in the staff, amongst other concerns?* Additional questions can be raised revealing the emotional process of a system choosing a poorly differentiated leader.

Poorly differentiated leaders weaken and diminish systems

Knowing about a system's emotional process is key to leadership excellence and satisfaction. The emotional process does not operate at the conscious level, at least not until persons are empowered to do so. Leaders who *know* about family systems theory and various forms of emotional reactivity are not guaranteed to lead differently. Consistently, our experience is that leaders with some systems theory knowledge are often most dangerous, for they think they can address the system's dynamics through charisma and their rational prowess. *Who then is the leader who can see the emotional process, remain less anxious, and initiate second-order change while remaining responsive to systemic reactions?* That person is the self-differentiated leader.

"Global leaders require an exceptionally high capacity for managing uncertainty," consultants Stewart Black and Allen Morrison write. "In some ways, they have to act like a juggler as they take on this challenge. Juggling is having more objects than hands."[1] The self-differentiated leader, being less anxious, does not reactively grab an object to juggle. Rather, some objects are best left to fall to the ground. A leader's success is certainly co-determined by their education, expertise, skill, and experience. Though these aspects can help any leader, they rarely translate into excellent leadership. Friedman, a seasoned leadership consultant, identifies *self-definition* and *self-differentiation* as the first steps toward effective leadership. Both dynamics imply engaging the emotional system differently.[2] Friedman defines self-differentiation as

> the capacity ... to define [one's] life's goals and values apart from surrounding togetherness pressures; to say *"I"* when others are demanding *"you"* or "we." It includes the capacity to maintain a (relatively) non-anxious presence amid anxious systems, to take maximum responsibility for one's destiny and emotional being. It can be measured somewhat by the breadth of one's repertoire of responses when confronted with a crisis.[3]

A self-differentiated leader remains less anxious—a term we prefer to being "nonanxious"—when others and the system itself are anxious and tension-filled. It is the leader who can moderate the degree of fusion with or differentiation from a system's emotional process. The leader whose self is strong enough to resist compliance to emotional manipulation.[4] The differentiated leader is not without heart and can express compassion and care while making difficult decisions. They know early experiences in their family of origin can have a direct effect on their current leadership expression.

Zach, the nonprofit leader we named in the Introduction, is a self-differentiated leader. He is successful in a challenging industry; he exudes personal confidence without arrogance, but rather with a deep humility; his empowered staff grows under his leadership; others seek him out as a mentor; he is a buffer between powerful stakeholders and his staff; he is less anxious, always responsive (and mindful not to become reactive), and remains open to change. What Zach rarely discloses is that he had a mentor, the person who started the nonprofit he now leads, and who taught him much of what he knows. She was a remarkable woman able to bring out the best in others while changing her city and community. Self-differentiated leaders often have mentors and teachers who help them grow out of their family of origin, i.e., they empower the leader to leave behind anxious ways of being and relating first learned in their family of origin. Think of managing conflict. If you did not grow up in a home where adults modeled effective communication in angry moments, but possibly stormed around or retreated in silence, where would you have learned how to stay present and nonreactive in moments of disagreement and high tension?

Feel when others want you to think; think when others want you to feel

A succinct definition of self-differentiation is *the ability to feel when others want you to think and to think when others want you to feel.* It is a person who can recognize forces pulling together or driving individuality, seeking conflict, yet remain steady in their stance and communication. It is near impossible for a person to be self-differentiated as a professional, yet remain poorly differentiated as a family member and as a member of society. We bring ourselves to every context we find ourselves in. Bowen, Friedman, and family therapists argue the journey to self-differentiation always begins with the persons closest to you, in the family that raised you or the family or families you created. This is true, but remember the emotional process permeates systems, and due to the interwoven nature of the process, one can begin one's self-differentiation in any system one is a part of. Self-differentiation always is a courageous and difficult path to choose. Many leaders who claim natural abilities to lead, pointing to their numerous degrees and deep experience, or who see leadership as a cognitive-rational practice, will find self-differentiation elusive.

Evonne's executives sought to diminish the impact of the choices they made. As they offered the simplistic solution of increased resilience within employees and remembered past challenges, Evonne felt the staff's experiences—their frustration, uncertainty, loss, anger, and even despair. As others felt hopeful she would change the system for good, she offered many scenarios of what failure might look like, even sharing her self-doubt. When some sought to vent in secret, Evonne was careful to be transparent in her communication.

The Challenge of Self-differentiation

The challenge around self-differentiation is threefold: First, one rarely thinks of oneself as being self-differentiated. It takes the hard work of redefining one's positions, roles, and functions in core relationships. Containing emotion and not becoming reactive is not a natural human stance. Redefining relationships and containing emotion are not abstract exercises. The mind often seeks easy ways out of challenging work and convinces us we can think ourselves into a new way of being. We are emotional beings first before we are rational. In our teaching, leadership, and consultation, we consistently find rational leaders devouring knowledge, accumulating data, engaging theories, quoting leadership gurus, and drafting new vision statements are less likely to grow in self-differentiation. We have seen students writing doctoral-length theses on self-differentiated leadership without showing any outward signs their leadership style has become less anxious.

Self-differentiation asks questions rational or data analysis cannot easily answer: *What work of self-differentiation do I need to do in my family of origin? What are my personal and professional goals, and how can I achieve those goals even as I lead my team or institution toward institutional goals? How can I be part of the system and remain an individual, a "me?" Or conversely, how can I have distance from my institution, yet remain part of it?* And, *when do I resign my executive functioning to the expectation and reactivity of the emotional process, and when I do so, at what personal and professional cost?* Sometimes a system is not ready for transformation. The members of the system need to wrestle a bit longer with their challenges and ways of being together before they are ready to grow to a higher level of functioning.

Second, self-differentiation demands differentiating from one's family of origin and in one's close intimate relationships. If we are stuck in our relationships with our parents, siblings, partners, or the members of the family we created, we diminish the possibility of mature, authentic, and ethical relationships in our professional relationships. Since human nature includes congruency, we present ourselves in similar ways across the spheres of life. Taking a new position in a relationship often includes speaking to a person or redefining the relationship one has with an internalized relationship. The latter opens the possibility of changing a relationship with an important loved one even after death. Sometimes self-differentiation includes reframing a relationship with a group, even one's history. Furthermore, the process of self-differentiation is not determined by the response of another person. It is about the position you take, not the other person's response or reactivity. You might thus seek to bridge the distance between you and a family member, even one refusing to engage you. Technology can help one here as one can send a text message or email, not expecting any reply.

Third, self-differentiation is a challenge for all who do not accept the counterintuitive wisdom of the emotional process in contemporary corporate culture. In a corporate world where leadership revolves around titles and degrees, past positions and experience, data, egos, compensation, and prestige, self-differentiation rarely makes the list of leadership attributes. Furthermore, as institutions wrestle with long histories of gender and racial inequalities and other intersectional legacies of injustice, we see poorly differentiated persons called into leadership. These leaders inevitably bring little change as family systems theory would predict for any poorly differentiated leader. Let's be clear, we are not against needed efforts of diversity, equality, and inclusion. Self-differentiation, however, cannot be assumed in a leader, especially for one charged to bring change the system is likely to resist and undermine. We believe all leaders with a high level of self-differentiation will facilitate the change they are tasked to bring.

A self-differentiated leader cannot be assumed

Poorly differentiated leaders are easily recognized. They:

■ Are distant or enmeshed in their personal relationships, which can be conflict-filled, void of intimacy, or easily break apart.
■ Neglect their professional goals, which may be vague or remain the same for years.
■ Self-medicate their stress.
■ Fall into groupthink, especially in moments of stress and conflict, and are easily influenced by other voices or trends.
■ Cause tension around them through poor discernment, stonewall when a situation has to be addressed, and portray contempt for others.
■ Deny mistakes made, easily pass blame and/or shame, and rarely apologize (perceived signs of weakness).
■ Seek to control, actively or passively, the choices and behaviors of others; some become authoritarian.
■ Present immature dependency needs and seek the acceptance, approval, and praise of others.
■ Tumble into irrational, emotionally driven decision-making, especially in moments of crisis.
■ Exhibit deep insecurities, especially when their competence or sense of belonging as a leader is challenged.
■ Poorly differentiated leaders find themselves stuck in their professional relationships or tasks, feeling overwhelmed by the various emotional processes around them, and can feel or be isolated.

The Self-differentiation Scale[5]

Bowen provides a self-differentiation scale, a mirror of sorts in which a leader can discover themselves anew (see Table 3.1). It is a map pointing them to greater levels of maturity and excellence. At the one end of the differentiation scale are those leaders whose emotions and intellects are fused to the emotional process. Their reactivity, assuring poor leadership, is a constant trait. The differentiated self is a secure self, able to withstand the pressure with clearly defined beliefs, incorporating convictions, opinions, and principles into the self in a congruent manner. This self will take responsible action according to these internalized principles. The differentiated leader can say: "This is who I am, what I believe, what I stand for, and what I will do or will not do in a given situation."[6]

Due to human nature, it is impossible to be 100% self-differentiated. To claim such a feat, one has to have levels of awareness and relations not humanly possible. We can, however, become increasingly self-differentiated. We certainly do not seek to be a poorly differentiated leader who is constantly vulnerable to the emotional pressures of anxiety. Imagine the life and leadership of a person who is principle-oriented and goal-directed, who self-directs their attention with confident assertiveness and self-regulation. And imagine the life and leadership of a person who needs to be loved by others and thus avoids conflict and keeps porous boundaries, who is vulnerable to the opinions of others or becomes rigid or rebellious when challenged. Under whose leadership would you rather serve? Which leader would you rather be?

Every leader finds themselves somewhere on Bowen's scale. More important than "achieving" a certain level, however, is you constantly engaging in the personal and relational work needed to move up on the scale. Excellent leaders are not necessarily the ones scoring in the 85–95 range, though those leaders are very likely to be excellent. Rather, *excellence in leadership is best understood as constantly doing the work needed to move higher on the scale, experiencing anxiety at a lower level than others in the system, and broadening one's repertoire to be responsive to a system in need of change.* A leader with a lower score but working toward deeper self-differentiation will be more effective at bringing change than a poorly differentiated leader with much authority or a leader who had a higher score in the past but who gave up on increasing their self-differentiation. A leader stuck in place is in reality regressing, a process their team or institution will follow.

As you approach the scale:

1. Read through the scale once. Since more detail is provided for the higher levels, adjust accordingly as the level of differentiation declines.
2. Imagine a leader you admire and plot them on the differentiation scale by looking carefully at the traits described.
3. Repeat the exercise by taking a leader you view as ineffective and also plot them on the scale.
4. Now you are familiar with two different levels of self-differentiation, take an honest assessment of your leadership. Plot yourself on the scale, mindful of any defensive reactivity the exercise awakens in you. Do not be surprised if you discover your level is lower than you anticipated.

Table 3.1   The Self-differentiation Scale

100	• Hypothetical/ideal human
85–95	• Very well differentiated. • Principle-oriented and goal-directed. • Inner-directed, internal locus of control, self-sufficient, self-regulating, assertive. • Not likely to be emotionally reactive. • Low anxiety; less anxious. • Not dogmatic or rigid in thinking and action. • A realistic self-image including realistic expectations and limitations of the self. • Secure in silence and values time in solitude.

(Continued)

Table 3.1 (Continued)   The Self-differentiation Scale

	• Functioning and self-image are not affected by praise or criticism. Welcomes and values honest feedback. • Can tolerate intense feelings. Has well-developed emotional skills and literacy. • At peace. Well-developed spirituality (not necessarily religious). • Not overly responsible for others. Does not need to micro-manage. • Not preoccupied with their place in the hierarchy. • Expectations of others are realistic. • Free to enjoy relationships; Does not have a "need" for others and others do not feel used. • Respect and value differences; Listen with an open mind. • Embraces change; Can discard old beliefs in favor of new ones. • Listens without reacting. • Communicates without antagonizing others. • Welcoming and warm, not non-adversarial or prone to engage in polarized debates. • Adapts in stressful situations without developing stress but will avoid such situations where there is a choice. • Excellent personal boundaries.
75	• Fairly well differentiated. • Can be calm in troubled times. • Moves between emotional closeness and independent goals. • More authentic—does not seek approval. • Less emotional reactivity and, if triggered, recovers quickly. • More choice between feelings and intellect. • Good boundaries.

(Continued)

Table 3.1 (Continued) The Self-differentiation Scale

60	• Acts more based on reason and intellect than simply reacting to feelings. • Considers and chooses actions rather than simply reacting to a feeling. • Thinks for self rather than simply following the opinions of others. • In relationships hesitates to say what he/she thinks. Can hide true thoughts/feelings/needs. • Boundary keeping is improving.
50	• Somewhat differentiated. • Principle-oriented and goal-directed at times. • Oscillates between being inner-directed or reactive to external forces. • If triggered or stressed, remains in that state for some time. • At peace or anxious depending on the circumstances. • Can be dogmatic and rigid in thought and action. • Seek to project an unrealistic view of the self; work at hiding limitations. • Feels lonely at times and finds solitude challenging. • Functioning and self-image, in anxious moments, are affected by praise or criticism. • Does not generally seek or value honest feedback. • Becomes rational when emotions become a burden. • Poorly developed spirituality (not necessarily religious). • Feels responsible for others. Tends to micromanage in anxious moments. • Is aware of their place in the hierarchy. • Carries unrealistic expectations of others. • Lacks time and space to enjoy relationships. • "Needs" others at times, who can feel used. • Becomes anxious when listening to differences; tries to convince others to adopt new thoughts.

(Continued)

Table 3.1 (Continued)   The Self-differentiation Scale

	• Knows change is inevitable, yet gets anxious when change arrives or is expected; discards old beliefs in favor of new ones with some difficulty. • Becomes reactive when listening. • Often antagonizes others when communicating; can be adversarial and polarizing. • Becomes anxious in stressful moments and emotionally distances, enmeshes, triangulates, or gets caught in conflict. • Has poor personal boundaries. • If triggered or stressed recovers less easily.
40	• Poorly differentiated. • Portrays a lifelong pursuit of ideal closeness or relationships. • Relationships tend to be based on mutual dependency, on being transactional, or might be avoided altogether. • Operates out of a pseudo-self/adapted inner child. Low level of the real self. • Often seeks the approval of others. Preoccupied with creating a good impression. • Feels good if affirmed, and bad if criticized/disapproved of. Self-image depends on outside feedback. • Influenced by feelings—low ability to choose actions rationally. • Poor emotional skill/literacy. • Poor or inconsistent boundaries. • Seeks distractions from self.
30	• Spends a lot of energy on "loving" or "being loved." • Highly suggestible to views/opinions of others and adopts viewpoints of others. Poor boundaries. • Prone to joining cults, sects, or adopting extremist or rigid black/white ideologies and philosophies; embrace conspiracy theories. • Alternatively, consistently rebellious or rigid in beliefs and views. • Successful at work only if praised by superiors.

(Continued)

Table 3.1 (Continued)   The Self-differentiation Scale

0–25	• Very poorly differentiated. • Most of the life energy goes into "loving" or "being loved" — most of the person's energy is consumed by reactiveness to having failed to get love. • Lives in a feeling world — but could also be so sensitive to the point of being emotionally numb. • High levels of chronic anxiety — difficult to find situations in which they can be truly comfortable. • Difficulty maintaining long-term relationships; gives up on relationships. • Emotionally needy and highly reactive to others. Co-dependent. No boundaries. • Little energy left for goal-directed pursuits — trying to achieve comfort is enough. • Functioning is almost entirely governed by emotional reactions to the environment. • Inability to differentiate between thoughts and feelings — isn't aware of alternatives to what they feel. • Responses range from automatic compliance to extreme oppositional behavior. • Very rarely, if ever, uses I-statements, such as: "I believe ...; I am ...; I will do ... I feel ...."

Placing a leader you observed and experienced is easier than self-assessing. *Where on the scale do you plot yourself? What internal reactions did you have, including defensive thoughts, as you read through the list and placed yourself and others on a spectrum? What work can you identify for yourself to increase your level of self-differentiation?*

The self-differentiation scale is self-evident. A leader who is at level 50 fundamentally leads differently compared to a leader higher or lower on the scale. Remember, the scale is not determined by one's level of education, experience, or even accolades or compensation. A poorly differentiated leader, as the case study opening this chapter indicated, can reach high levels of office and be effective at some aspects of leadership. Leadership, however, demands much more than doing one or two things well.

Leadership consultant Peter Steinke finds that differentiated leaders impact their systems by

- "separating themselves from the surrounding anxiety
- making decisions based on principle, not instinct
- taking responsibility for their emotional being
- regulating their anxiety in the face of sabotage or resistance
- staying connected to others, even those who disagree with them ...
- focusing on emotional processes rather than the symptoms they produce ... [and]
- accepting that mature leadership does not always work, that immaturity is too embedded in the system."[7]

An organization's health is determined by the level of self-differentiation of especially its top leadership. Organizations investing in leadership to grow vis-à-vis the emotional process increase the possibility of growing and being successful.

Self-differentiation as Managing Relationships in Discomfort, i.e., Anxiety

Though we can distinguish the differentiated leader from the leader who is not differentiated, constructs such as "emotional process" and "self-differentiation" can remain abstract. To concretize these constructs, family therapists refer to "pain" or "struggle" and "closeness" or "distance" in relationships

(Figure 3.1). Here, "pain" and "struggle" indicate the physical, emotional, financial, and ethical anxieties our personal and relational lives can experience. Being self-differentiated increases one's threshold in the presence of pain and struggle; one can maintain an emotional closeness to others even as one sees them in discomfort. It is walking toward one's concerns or the concerns of others when the natural tendency is to remain in denial or to withdraw from the relationship. When a leader remains apathetic toward their personal or relational troubles and is greatly affected by the anxiety of others, it soon becomes an unbearable burden for the leader. For poorly differentiated leaders, the uncomfortableness fuels either underfunctioning—not tending to personal concern—or overfunctioning—doing the emotional, relational, and even professional work of the other person (see Chapter 2). Should a leader be either enmeshed with others or try to lead from a distance—possibly by claiming power over others since no relationship exists to facilitate change—no transformation can be expected.

Between being on the path of burnout and facing failure, a poorly differentiated leader has to rely on other defense mechanisms to sustain themselves and to create the illusion of change. The concepts and reality of pain and struggle invite a leader to be present to suffering, discomfort, or dysfunction, recognizing what is going on, but refraining from "fixing" persons or systems, which would be an act of overfunctioning. Remember, you are part of the system and thus inherently part of the problem. Through self-differentiation you give yourself and the systems you are a part of a chance to move toward a new position of health and functioning. Due to systemic interdependence, one's ability to remain present in difficult situations increases the same ability in others.

Self-differentiated leaders never try to fix people or systems

Seeing self-differentiation through the lenses of pain, struggle, closeness, and distance implies that a leader typically functions from one of four stances:

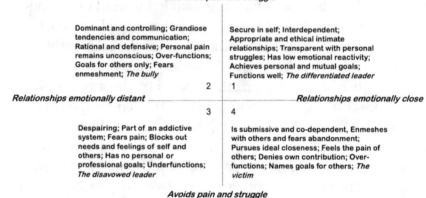

Leadership orientations

Embraces pain and struggle

Dominant and controlling; Grandiose tendencies and communication; Rational and defensive; Personal pain remains unconscious; Over-functions; Goals for others only; Fears enmeshment; *The bully*	Secure in self; Interdependent; Appropriate and ethical intimate relationships; Transparent with personal struggles; Has low emotional reactivity; Achieves personal and mutual goals; Functions well; *The differentiated leader*
2	1

Relationships emotionally distant ——————————————————— *Relationships emotionally close*

3	4
Despairing; Part of an addictive system; Fears pain; Blocks out needs and feelings of self and others; Has no personal or professional goals; Underfunctions; *The disavowed leader*	Is submissive and co-dependent, Enmeshes with others and fears abandonment; Pursues ideal closeness; Feels the pain of others; Denies own contribution; Over-functions; Names goals for others; *The victim*

Avoids pain and struggle

Figure 3.1   Embracing pain or struggle and remaining emotionally connected.

The leader in Block #1, having grown considerably toward being self-differentiated, is secure enough to engage what is experienced as "pain" and "struggle" in their personal and relational lives. They can do so while maintaining healthy closeness to others. This leader pursues personal goals, creates mutual goals, and is attractive to others as the system changes toward health. Being self-differentiated implies owning your decisions have real-life implications for others from which you are protected.

The leader in Block #2 is the leader whose narcissistic traits are so strong that they lean toward the pathological side. It is the charismatic leader who communicates effectively and offers a vision of an ideal community or institution. This leader is never a team player but can call forth a cult-like following. They know how to exploit persons and resources. The leader in Block #2 is often guilty of sins of commission—of acting in ways that bring change, but not change serving the greater good. Bullying, after all, can change the dynamics on a playground, but soon the children will leave to play elsewhere.

The leader in Block #3 avoids their pain and struggles and is uncomfortable seeing others struggling, thus underfunctions inward and distances outward. Their sin is the sin of omission. With no personal goals to achieve and becoming anxious in the presence of others' pain and struggles, this leader will be reluctant to act and disavowing. Why would this person become a leader? Since systems choose their leaders, any system resisting change will find this kind of leader perfect for their system. Other times a system needs an interim leader, someone who will not remain in leadership long. This often happens after a leader with a long tenure leaves, or a leader leaves under a dark cloud. Since no change is likely to occur, the system can breathe a sigh of relief and lick its wounds.

The leader of Block #4 has a keen awareness of the pain and struggles of others, and of what needs to be changed. This leader, however, lacks personal goals, and their pain functions mostly on an unconscious level. Since personal pain and struggles are ego-dystonic—the self does not seek to be in an unsettled, anxious state—the discomfort is projected onto others. Filled with anxiety (now projected outward), the leader becomes co-dependent and submissive, willing to do anything to alleviate a person's or system's anxieties. It is the leader whose team does not come through on a presentation and then will work all night to do the team's work. Imagine the leader who will assist others financially but then becomes frustrated when the resources are squandered. It is the leader who feels abandoned when a team member resigns. If a leader denies or overestimates someone's personal and professional responsibilities, the threshold for pain and the ability to be a responsible agent decline.[8]

Hidden in the self-differentiation scale above are thus relationships either close or distant, and a specific orientation vis-à-vis pain, struggle, and discomfort. *In which block would you place the wise, effective leader you identified assessing their self-differentiation?* Our guess is in Block #1. *And where would you place the leader you experienced as poorly differentiated?* Blocks #2–4? *In which quadrant do you place yourself?* Excellent leaders are constantly working toward Block #1 or seeking to deepen the traits represented by the block. Engaging in this book will help you do so.

As stated, contemporary leadership often hides behind and relies upon data, which is very different from the self-differentiated leader who can engage in the emotional process of a system. Differentiated leaders are not against the use of data. No, they engage with data differently and can do so since they remain less anxious in conversations. They can ask more probing questions since data is only as good as the data points included and its interpretation, which opens data to bias and shortcomings. Few moments in leadership rival the tension awakened when the same data is used to support two opposing ideas, as one often find in politics.

Self-differentiated Leaders Use Data Differently

Imagine you are driving a car, possibly the sports model you always coveted, or a classic car elevating every garage. Everything in the vehicle works as expected—except you cannot see out of the front or side windows. You can see only via the rear-view mirror and therefore through the rear window of the vehicle. Not even the side mirrors are available to you. You are sitting facing backward driving forward. The only road you can see, therefore, is the road you have just traveled. *How far will you get driving the vehicle in this manner?*

Of course, much will depend on the road in front of you. If the road does not change from the section you just covered, if it is straight, for example, or follows the same curve, then it is totally practical to drive your car by looking through the rearview mirror. If, however, the road suddenly curves or if there are obstacles in your way, you'll have a problem. It is highly likely you'll crash into something or leave the road. Even if the road ahead is straight and there is a low probability of obstacles, you will likely continue at a slow speed with time-consuming progress. You may be too late for events you looked forward to. *Our reliance on data is like driving a car while looking only at the rear-view mirror.*

We certainly don't recommend you try driving by looking only at the rearview mirror, and we trust this brief thought experiment is sufficient to make our point a leader, without the ability to engage in the emotional process of determining all possibilities for change, will become stuck or crash, sooner or later. Increasingly, leaders are data-driven, using the data both to make their decisions and to boost their egos. One can argue leadership has been reduced to data gathering and interpretation. Data represents the past and denies the emotional process since data rarely is curious about how systems function. Data are extremely vulnerable to data points used or excluded and how the interpretation of the data is understood and done. Biases easily creep into interpretation. Furthermore, numbers—data—poorly, at best, describe relationships, a person's position in a system, their role and function, or the emotional process.

Perhaps we should take lessons from leaders in the pharma, biotech, and medical devices industries, who, to bring a new medication or product to market, must achieve a statistically significant result in multiple randomized double-blinded clinical trials to demonstrate the efficacy and safety of a new product. Would you want to take, or advise others to take, medications or use medical devices approved by the FDA based on *directionally correct* rather than *statistically valid results?* Most likely, you work or have worked for an organization with many workers who rely on directional data. Differentiated leaders have learned that data analyses can often present tempting conclusions that evaporate over time. As you read conclusions supported by data analysis, take note of whether or not the results of any such analyses are statistically valid, e.g., $p < 0.05$. Leaders typically have to make do with the data and analyses at hand, for what they are and are not worth.

When you use data, recognize you are dealing with the road just traveled, not the road ahead or the emotional process of the system. Knowing one's past is important, and our argument for a model helping a leader use data differently does not deny such data can play an important role in a leader's discernment processes. No. We're arguing core leadership skills include self-differentiation and the ability to use data wisely to understand a system's emotional process.

A leader can impact the future in infinite ways

The siren call of data is attractive and can easily become the go-to resource for leaders. As data storage and computational speeds increase exponentially, we have almost infinite opportunities to analyze data and trends. The raw amounts of data available increase the likelihood of leaders being overwhelmed to the point of paralysis. Furthermore, the interpretation of data exposes our biases, as we see in algorithms discriminating against women, persons of color, persons from different religious and political perspectives, even persons with different abilities. It is difficult to fathom how, with the same data sets, even experts come to conclusions that are polar opposites, leaving unbridgeable chasms between viewpoints. Wise leaders regard data, its use, the findings, and the recommended actions from the data with appropriate skepticism. We tend to use data to serve an existing emotional process, which remains unexplored and may need serious change. As one documentary states: "We have almost infinite data about the past yet have no way to impact it. We have no data about the future but have infinite ways to impact it."[9]

Holding coexisting truths—forms of data that may or may not oppose each other—is something a differentiated leader can do as they facilitate change for their system. As the emotional process reacts to change, soon coexisting truths will surface as groups coalesce around certain (often opposing) ideas. *Accepting coexisting truths or realities* means acknowledging polar opposite positions or opinions might both be true. It asks a leader to refrain from questioning whether statements are true or false since they will never know or be able to collect enough data to confirm the truth. Leaders who accept coexisting truths acknowledge each truth and assess its implications for their institution. They draw extensively on their self-differentiation, which allows them to be less anxious in a system.

Often poorly differentiated leaders or organizations, companies, and political parties with a dysfunctional emotional process become stuck or polarized in an opinion or belief. They take a polarized position and can only see one path forward into the future. We can readily name companies or organizations that became stuck around an issue or product: Kodak and digital photography; Blockbuster and video rentals; car dealerships and online motor vehicle sales; faith communities and LGBTQIA+ persons marrying; or in-person education and virtual, online instruction. Saying institutions get stuck is a half-truth, for prior to getting stuck, the emotional process within the system and the poorly differentiated leaders of these institutions were stuck first. Stuckness leads to unproductive behavior as arguments ensue but also inevitable market decline, aggressive takeovers, and on the international scale, arms races and wars. Leaders whose data interpretation led them to poor decisions abound.

One revered historic leader in Israel's history could accept coexisting truths. From 970 to 931 BCE, King Solomon, who followed his father, King David, ruled over Israel.[10] Two women who both claimed they were the mothers of the same child came to him embroiled in conflict, hoping King Solomon would side with one against the other. Both became mothers at the same time, but one mother's child died. The other mother said the mother who lost her infant exchanged her deceased baby for the surviving, healthy baby. The other woman vehemently denied the exchange and said the dead infant belonged to the mother who now claims her son was stolen.

Without modern techniques like DNA testing, how could King Solomon solve this problem? Both women presented compelling and heartfelt arguments that the surviving child was theirs. King Solomon could have embarked on a journey to collect as much data as possible to try and prove which woman was the mother. Interviews, witnesses, finding the fathers, family members, and the midwives who helped birth the children—these sources could all have testified as to which mother was speaking the truth. King Solomon, however, would be no closer to the truth if the different sources supported each of the two women as the mother of the surviving baby. One can see King Solomon getting stuck and the polarization continuing.

Polarization = emotional distancing = being stuck

Known for his wisdom, King Solomon did not go on a fact-finding mission but accepted the testimony of both mothers. He took them down a different path, a direction no one had anticipated as a way to solve the problem. King Solomon's acceptance of two truths presented him with an alternative solution.

The narrative tells that:

> The king said, "This one says, 'My son is alive and your son is dead.' The other one says, 'No! Your son is dead and my son is alive.' Get me a sword!" They brought a sword to the king. Then the king said, "Cut the living child in two! Give half to one woman and half to the other woman." Then the woman whose son was still alive said to the king, "Please, Your Majesty, give her the living child; please don't kill him," for she had a great love for her son. But the other woman said, "If I can't have him, neither will you. Cut the child in half." Then the king answered, "Give the first woman the living newborn. Don't kill him. She is his mother.

In a verdict sounding strange to our ears, King Solomon ordered the baby to be cut in half and half be given to each mother. Immediately, he increased the anxiety in the system. Offered this solution, one of the mothers immediately abdicated any right to the child, preferring to see the child live. She was willing to let the other women have the child without question, exposing herself as the real mother. Problem solved, the argument ended.

King Solomon decided that the woman who wanted to see the child live was the real mother, and therefore he gave the child to her. Did he know for sure that she was the mother? He had no empirical evidence to prove her maternity. So the honest answer is: no, he did not know this was the birth

mother of the child. Perhaps he was not interested in proving which one was the birth mother, but was more interested
in determining which one would make the best mother.
Accepting that both women were telling the truth created
an alternative path, one that neither mother expected. King
Solomon was able to remove himself from the gridlock and
the argument and create an alternative way forward. Note that
King Solomon did not use compromise as a new path.

It is counterintuitive to accept two coexisting truths
at the same time. Few leaders model for us this capacity.
Furthermore, our religions, moral codes, and ethics are all
built on dichotomous conceptions of right and wrong, good
and evil, or heaven and hell. When we take a position on
something and perceive it to be true, it is hard to let go of that
belief. One's vantage point determines whether what we see
will be two persons' profiles or a vase. Defending one truth
in the light of another awakens anxiety in ourselves and others, and we then feel a need to defend against the anxiety by
becoming passive-aggressive, distancing ourselves, or by entering into conflict. Since the anxiety is impossible to contain, it
flows into the system of which we are a part, and soon the
whole system reverberates with anxiety.

History is littered with truths proved false: the earth is
flat, the sun revolves around the earth, the universe had
no beginning, and the atom is the smallest known particle.
Think about personal pain, societal conflicts, and even international wars caused by individuals, groups, and countries
who defended one truth against another. Accepting coexisting
truths unshackles us from our biases, our politics, our religions, and our political beliefs. It allows us to look at the other
side of an argument or hypothesis and consider both the good
and the bad implications of the alternatives being true. Self-
differentiated leaders can lead others to new possibilities by
remaining less anxious as opposite truths are explored.

Politics Is Driven by Opposite Truths

The ever-polarizing political debates in the United States are good examples of opposing truths being offered. Despite significant amounts of information and data, different media sources come to different and often polar-opposite conclusions. The dynamics are such that, irrespective of the topic or theme under discussion, the dichotomized result remains the same. For mere mortals, it is almost impossible to decipher the information being presented.

In the early days of contemplating this book, America was wrestling with Russian influence in American politics and elections, with some faulting fellow Americans for colluding with "the Russians" (who have become a monolithic group). Using a political example can be risky, but few commitments unleash more passion and opinions than political commitments. One side believed this was how an election was lost, and had it not been for Russian interference, they would be in charge. The other side believed we were witnessing a deep state reacting to change entering the system. Each of us, like King Solomon, was confronted with a barrage of conflicting information and reporting. Each side had its way to present, pursue, conflate, and manipulate information to bolster its side of the argument. News media, following the nation's emotional process, took sides.

A self-differentiated leader would be less interested in the "truth" of the possible interference since data can be interpreted in many ways. The challenge was real: Does the information being presented suggest the President of the United States is working with or for Russia, or is there a corrupt intelligence organization working with the left to overthrow the US government? Imagine the time and resources wasted if the former question was only a tactic to distract one's political adversary and the latter question a countermeasure in the extreme.

Countless hours of reporting in the news media, a year-long special investigation, and even congressional hearings led to no consensus. Folks on either side of the political divide heard the facts they wanted to hear. Trying to unpack the reasoning behind each group to find a common truth was and still is an exercise in futility. Feeling overwhelmed by all the diverse reporting, people reverted to their (biased) previously held positions. The political divide became deeper still, or at least nothing much changed.

What do you think: Should you aim to be a neutral leader, listening to both sides and hoping to reach a rational conclusion? Should you persuade one group to accept the truth of the other group? The pursuit and presentation of the "facts" are likely to leave you and those you lead paralyzed. *How can you possibly make an informed decision in a sea of opposing data?* As you become stuck as a leader, those around you will experience your stuckness as a leadership void. The most anxious around you will step into this void to assume leadership, a direct challenge to your poorly differentiated leadership.

What we witness at the political level is no different than what happens in our organizations, departments, and companies. The system's anxiety, driven by the opposing data and by the reactivity to the leadership void created, propels others to step in and claim leadership. They can create an opportunity for revolutions. As a leader, this is where you need to be more like King Solomon. You need to rise above the anxiety and gridlock, think forward by accepting both arguments to be true, and see what bends in the road appear. Do so without judging the different assertions made. There is no value in trying to prove either hypothesis. By accepting both positions to be absolutely true, you can then decide what the implications of both being true might be.

First, we'll consider whether the president is indeed working for Russia. Think this through: What does this mean practically, and what scope does Russia have to affect the United States if they have control of the president? Imagine the possibilities. Once you have fully thought this through without questioning the position's validity, you can then turn your attention to the alternative hypothesis, the deep-state argument. With equal clarity and lack of bias, you should think through what the implications are of this position being true.

To accept the data in support of Russian collusion, we need to know what Russia's foreign and domestic policies or priorities are and how the president might help Russia achieve these. We can ask:

1. What are the president's incentives to be working for Russia?
2. How would Russia reward the president for working for him?
3. What leverage does Russia have over the president to keep him in line and continue to work for Russia?
4. How does the president communicate with Russia in ways that avoid national intelligence?
5. What executive orders can the president enact on behalf of Russia doesn't require a constitutional review of control, that doesn't have to pass through the House and Senate?

One possible answer to the last question is that the president can order an attack on a foreign nation without the approval of the rest of the US government. You could argue that this is something a foreign power could exploit. So, if we change the rules so that the president has to get approval from the branches of government, this would surely lower the risk of any foreign country collusion argument. It does not have to be the current president and Russia; you could accept this argument to be true either now or at any time in the future and about any President and any foreign country. It is plausible that it could be true in the future, if not true now.

What leverage might Russia have over the presidency? Perhaps Russia has access to secrets from the past that it could use to blackmail the president. The president might be embarrassed or trapped and not want this information shared. This gives Russia influence over his thinking. Again let's just accept this to be true. Would a good policy be to hold US presidents harmless to foreign claims while they are holding office? Both parties are likely to agree that blackmail by a foreign power puts the entire country at risk. Should the US press agree not to publish stories from foreign sources on an individual who is a sitting president? Would these kinds of laws and principles help to protect the US?

Is it more worthwhile pursuing activities limiting or neutralizing a foreign power's influence rather than trying to prove whether they are colluding with the president? You can continue to run down the list of implications of the collusion argument, accepting them to be true, and then work on eliminating their impact. You might reach a point where even if a president were being influenced by a foreign power, the checks and balances in the system are such that it does not matter much. You could make a reasonable argument now that the US governing system is quite robust concerning a rogue leader. So even if the presidency were being influenced by a foreign power, the influence will be limited.

Let's now consider the deep-state argument. To accept the facts supporting the reality of a deep state seeking to undermine the presidency of the United States, we need to discern the implications of a corrupt intelligence agency that will not stop until it removes a democratically elected president. We can ask:

1. What are the implications of one political party working against the other through an intelligence agency?

2. What are the implications for citizens if the intelligence agencies use and abuse their power and are focused on overthrowing democratically elected officials?
3. Who holds intelligence agencies accountable?
4. Who protects the rights of the citizens?
5. How will a few deep state agents be able to manipulate all elected officials and the military leadership?
6. What are the implications of news media organizations serving the deep state?

Just as we have a Hippocratic oath for medical professionals, perhaps we should have a similar oath for journalists and reporters. In the movie *All the President's Men*, our intrepid reporters Bob Woodward (played by Robert Redford) and Carl Bernstein (played by Dustin Hoffman) "felt" they were right about Nixon. Often they would review their story, and their hypothesis, with their editor, Benjamin Bradlee, who continued to push them for more evidence to support their intuition. Bradlee was reluctant to harm or damage the reputation of the newspaper on their reporting hunch.[11]

Rather than trying to prove or disprove whether certain sectors of the media or news are participating in undermining our democracy, we could consider changing the rules of the game. If a newspaper is continually found to be publishing stories that are not true, inaccurate, and don't meet the standards we expect, should we close the newspaper? Like a Chapter 11 event for a badly run company, perhaps such newspapers should close or stop publishing, or publish fiction and comics. Maybe readers can revolt against companies who advertise and thus close off a definite income stream for the company.

Some people argue that intelligence agencies and law enforcement agencies have become partisan and actively work to undermine democracy and the democratic vote of the people. Let's accept this to be true. What would we do differently to limit the likelihood of this happening? Greater transparency on information that these agencies collect and use is the most common go-to solution. There are always counterarguments to this being done to protect security, protect the country. However, in almost every case it is only when information and documents become transparent that we have any chance of assessing what people are really doing and what their motivations are. Greater transparency and methods to make information more transparent are something we should all encourage and pursue. There is probably more upside benefit in this approach than downside risk of creating a security problem for the country.

Should people in intelligence agencies be allowed to vote? Should their voting and political donation records be made transparent? Should we be informed about their family of origin and political views within the family? Are there times when there is a conflict of interest if they investigate certain politicians or political activity? The reality of this truth of either collusion or a deep state is that it is much harder to regulate, control, or eliminate if it is true. By accepting both of these to be true, you might recognize that a deep state truth is far more concerning than collusion.

Like King Solomon, leaders can resist going on a fact-finding journey to find the truth. Often you will never be able to figure out the truth. So instead, consider the consequences of both scenarios being true and then decide which one you want the most or which one you want the least. Understanding which one might be the least desirable can help chart a path forward. Leaders can use this technique to help teams, departments, and business units resolve conflict when the data has failed to provide an obvious answer. If there are two or more possible truths, then accept each of them, in turn, to be true and think through the possible consequences of each.

Let's imagine your organization or business has a competitor taking away market share. Some team members see the competitor as a major threat, while others argue the opposite and recommend business as usual. In the metaphor we have been using in this chapter, you find yourself in a debate of whether the perception the competitor is a threat is true or not. Rather than taking up significant time in the boardroom or the leadership team meeting trying to debate this truth, try accepting both to be true. Accept both possibilities and think them through. What are the implications of each possibility? What do the scenarios being portrayed reveal? Remember, it might be worthless trying to decide which statement is true. *It is more important placing tests and controls for the least desirable* truth. As you do so, it is possible to change your position on the data, what data needs to be collected, how you are collecting data, and how you are validating "facts" in both truths. Equally, you can invest in the more desirable truth. How do you increase the chances of the desirable truth becoming a reality?

As we conclude this section on not getting stuck, let's briefly return to the argument for Russian collusion or the reality of a deep-state conspiracy. We remind ourselves presidents make very few decisions, despite the fear called forth in the image the president holds the keys to the US nuclear arsenal. The governance structures of the United States are well balanced with a legislative branch (the House of Representatives and the Senate), an executive branch (the president, vice-president, and cabinet), and a judicial branch (the federal judiciary). With these branches in place, it is almost impossible for the president to act independently or unilaterally. Even the executive decision of a president to go to war can be curtailed by the Senate. This being the case, and now we have accepted the collusion truth, an obvious action would be to change the president's executive authority. Rather than wasting time trying to prove whether there is collusion or not, just change this rule. Of course, we imagine politicians will balk at this suggestion. *How much time, money, and energy have been wasted on the collusion investigation? Would it have been easier just to change the executive authority on going to war?* Such a change would greatly reduce the exposure or risk of the collusion argument being true.

Nature knows opposites go together. Light is a wave and a particle. Life and leadership bring many moments where seemingly conflicting truths can leave one stuck. It happens in our intimate relationships, when team members poorly fit their positions, or when we try to enforce rules. Remaining less anxious and finding a way forward are important. It demands differentiated leadership.

Holding the Tension

Accepting coexisting truths and refraining from proving or disproving perceived truths can neutralize the power or implications of those truths. We do not suggest this is a leadership skill that comes naturally to a leader. Rather, most leaders exert much energy to solve the tension opposing ideas bring. Self-differentiated leaders, however, know otherwise. They can hold the tension opposite truths bring and can resist becoming reactive as they are pushed and pulled in different directions. Effective leaders find creative ways and methods, some explored here, to move an individual, a team, an organization, or a company beyond a polarized, stuck position. If you review the self-differentiation scale you'll see high self-differentiation characteristics like "Not prone to engage in polarizing debates," "low anxiety," and "can adapt under stress." These are all characteristics equipping a self-differentiated leader to operate with coexisting truths. Take someone low on the scale who "lives in a feeling world" and who functions almost entirely governed by emotional reactions to the environment. Such an individual will find it hard to coexist with opposed truths.

Not all people on your team will be individuals who can claim high levels of self-differentiation. It is important to have everyone participate in these forward-thinking or thinking-it-through exercises, regardless of their comfort in accepting coexisting truths. There is something therapeutic and validating for individuals to see their truth fully accepted and explored. Their voice is being heard and is always important in developing trust. Over time, you and your team will develop and improve your ability to engage with opposing data. Any initial passive stance is probably better than a highly disruptive stance in which persons refuse to give time to the alternative point of view, or worse, shout it down. You could argue that the passive stance is about halfway to being differentiated. Keep working with these individuals and help them develop to the point at which they feel comfortable exploring concepts and beliefs that so far have been alien to them.

Self-differentiated leaders are sought-after colleagues, mentors, and employees. Why? Because they:[12]

■ Participate in human flourishing.
■ Experience less anxiety and exuberance about life.
■ Project a sense of serenity.
■ Stick with things, even in difficult times.
■ Look at others with compassion in their hearts.
■ Acknowledge a certain holiness in people and creation.
■ Remain loyal to their commitments.
■ Hold power loosely. And, self-differentiated leaders.
■ Marshal and direct their energy wisely.

What kind of leader, colleague, and mentor do you seek to be?

Notes

1. J. Stewart Black and Allen J. Morrison, *The Global Leadership Challenge* (New York: Taylor & Francis, 2014), 105.
2. Friedman, *Generation to Generation: Family Process in Church and Synagogue*, 27.
3. Ibid.
4. Ibid., 362.

5. The scale is found in Kerr Bowen *Family Evaluation: An Approach Based on Bowen Theory* N: Norton 97–107. Here it is adapted and expanded from: http://www.fullyhuman.co.uk/wp-content/uploads/2012/08/Scale-of-differentiation-updated-2012-02-13.pdf. Accessed August 12, 2021.
6. Bowen, 164.
7. Peter L. Steinke, *Uproar: Calm Leadership in Anxious Times* (Lanham: Rowman & Littlefield, 2019), viii.
8. Friedman, *Generation to Generation: Family Process in Church and Synagogue*, 48.
9. Taken from the documentary, *What the Bleep to We Know*. See: https://whatthebleep.com/. Accessed September 4, 2021.
10. We read this court proceeding in *The Bible*, 1 Kings 3:16–28. For King Solomon, see: https://en.wikipedia.org/wiki/Solomon. Accessed August 17, 2021.
11. For a write-up on the movie, see: https://en.wikipedia.org/wiki/All_the_President%27s_Men_(film). Accessed August 17, 2021.
12. These traits were named by an early Jewish leader, the Apostle Paul c. 50–60 CE. See Galatians 5:22–23 in *The Bible*.

Chapter 4

Embracing Response-ability: Resisting Emotional Manipulation

How you respond to a situation is more determining than the ways any situation presents itself. Differentiated leaders know this intuitively as they witness vastly different responses to a work challenge. They see persons becoming enmeshed trying to get all to think and do alike, while others in their team or organization bring division. Some will refuse to be active participants toward a solution or change while others yet become embroiled in conflict. Friedman used the equation **HE = RO** to describe how emotional systems react and to underscore the importance of differentiated leadership. **HE** stands for the *hostility in an environment* or system. **RO**, in turn, indicates *the response of an organism*.[1] Effective leaders are not the heroes often worshipped by their followers. No, transformative leaders can manage hostility—resistance to change—when the emotional process and its members have become reactive.

DOI: 10.4324/9781003463993-7

Indeed, remaining less anxious when a situation turns challenging, even hostile, is challenging. Here, mentors, boards, and role models can empower a leader to grow in confidence when regressing to lower levels of self-differentiation can be expected. Certainly, leaders who work on their self-differentiation can find themselves in moments of being anxious. They too fall off the proverbial balance beam. However, differentiated leaders need not remain on the ground in a pool of anxiety for very long. A different way of leading is possible, one not flooding the self or system with anxiety.

Remaining responsive and less anxious opens the possibility of change

Hostile environments are filled with members unable to self-regulate their experience. Like a virus without an organizing capacity or a cancer growing without awareness of its home organism, poorly differentiated persons invade the lives of others—spaces—seeking to drive the emotional process. Online forums provide a rich atmosphere for this reactivity. Poor self-regulation goes together with a deep resistance to learning from experience. Regardless of the level of anxiety in a system, a leader can bring change, even if the only change is the leader being less anxious. After all, some systems are so stuck and hostile that only the most narcissistic leader can think they can bring change. That leader's low self-differentiation will thwart success.

How do you react when you are at the receiving end of hostility? How do you curb your defensiveness? How might your leadership change if you remain less anxious? Where in your leadership did you bring about change by doing something innovative, even unexpected? Self-differentiated leaders remain responsive and curb their reactivity.

The Fallacy of Empathy

Friedman tells of making a presentation that did not go as planned.[2] His topic was imaginative gridlock and the great sixteenth-century explorers which opened new worlds to all. Suddenly someone stood up and said Friedman's presentation was one of the most boring presentations he ever heard and he felt hurt by Friedman's ethnocentric bias—the West opening new worlds while colonizing lands and peoples. Friedman's response—remember he was a rabbi—must have surprised everyone: "I told him directly that I couldn't care less about his feelings and that I was trying to present universal, challenging ideas about the orientations of stuck civilizations and the evolutionary value of adventure."[3] Friedman reiterated what he set out to do in his presentation. Immediately another member of the audience came to the man's defense and stated Friedman was avoiding the man's feelings. Friedman responded by saying that focusing on feelings and bringing in political rhetoric veers attention away from the themes under discussion—stuck civilizations, how the emotional process mirrors natural processes, and how to bring change. Distinguishing feelings from opinions is crucial, Friedman stated.

Friedman portrayed much *chutzpah* to respond in a public presentation the way he did. Few of us would be able to follow him in his self-differentiation and remain less anxious in the face of public challenges. We can imagine a defensive leader, protecting their shame, challenging a team member, but there is a significant difference between challenging from a position of power and responding from a position of self-differentiation. The latter imagines a leader able to sustain a difficult conversation in a less anxious way. We imagine many in the audience listening to Friedman gasped when he told the man he could not care less about his feelings. He wanted to show how contemporary culture remains stuck despite the rhetoric of progress. Few may have caught that teaching.

"I have consistently found the introduction of the subject of 'empathy' into family, institutional, and community meetings to be reflective of, as well as an effort to induce, a failure of nerve among its leadership," Friedman writes.[4]

Friedman warns against the danger of *empathy*, being sensitive to emotional reactions of especially togetherness forces and the drive to individuality. Let's be clear, Friedman is not advocating being an obnoxious, cold leader:

- Friedman is not saying leaders should not acknowledge or be sympathetic to people's feelings.
- He is not saying feelings can be ignored or discounted for not being real or important to people.
- Friedman is not saying you should not support or help people who need help.

Rather, Friedman calls on a leader:

- To see things through regardless of how someone might feel.
- To resist being manipulated by the emotional reaction of another person or group.
- To identify attempts to sabotage the conversation or the process of discernment.
- To validate the experiences of others while communicating in "I-language," i.e., to communicate personal goals or an agreed-upon vision.

When a leader succumbs to emotional manipulation, a failure of nerve sets in. Systems and leaders feel deeply, but leading from an emotional place neither induces self-differentiation nor changes a system. An example might be a leader who delays making decisions since their team has already experienced a great deal of change, and the leader thinks the team cannot accept additional change. It is the leader who, despite a financial crisis, resists cutting salaries of the executive team alongside all other employees and does so without addressing the bigger financial challenges. Or the leader who avoids challenging conversations as they feel uncomfortable not being liked or challenged. The leader then quotes data few can challenge and fewer yet understand or call on procedures such as Robert's Rules of Order to force change, keeping things rational at all times.

Empathic leadership is more common than one might imagine. A review committee showed that a candidate did not meet specific job expectations. They continued to provide reasons as to why this had happened, ranging from the candidate's divorce and health concerns to institutional dysfunction that impacted the candidate. The committee highlighted community contributions the candidate made over the years, referenced issues of gender and race, and was generally sympathetic toward the candidate. The fact that the candidate never sought help from the institution's Employee Assistance Program and never indicated a struggle in meeting expectations went unmentioned. The fact that the neglected duties and expectations of the candidate negatively affected the lives of many was overlooked, even as it exposed a lack of holding persons responsible. The review committee's recommendation was to change the candidate's job description so that different criteria (and lower expectations) would be in place; also to hire an associate to assist the candidate. The leaders of the organization approved the changes as recommended, protecting a poorly functioning employee and revealing much about the institution's emotional process.

Empathic ways of leading fuel anxiety in the system as the system senses the crises, doubts the data, and wonders why some emotions (or people) are accepted or valued and others are not. Friedman states empathic decisions are inherently hostile, as they infuse the system with resentment, uncertainty, and anger.

Empathy—*to feel*—is a rather modern concept, entering the Oxford English Dictionary only in 1922. Its original meaning was projecting oneself into a piece of art so that those seeing or experiencing the art can better appreciate the piece. Empathy was reckoned more advanced than *sympathy*, to feel *the same*, for example. The adjective *empathic* only entered literature during World War II. It assumed projecting oneself into another's shoes would help us understand the other person better. Friedman, recognizing that challenging empathy sounds like blasphemy, sees the growth of empathy reflecting an increasingly anxious society over the last 60 odd years. He finds fault with what empathy has come to mean. "Empathy," Friedman concludes, "may be a luxury afforded only to those who do not have to make tough decisions."[5]

> On the one hand, there can be no question that the notion of feeling for others, caring for others, identifying with others, being responsive with others, and perhaps even sharing their pain exquisitely and excruciatingly is heartfelt, highly spiritual, and an essential component in a leader's response repertoire. But it has rarely been my experience that being sensitive to others will enable those "others" to be more self-aware, that being more "understanding" of others causes them to mature, or that appreciating the plight of others will make them more responsible for their being, their condition, or their destiny.[6]

Superficial need-fulfillment does not cultivate human flourishing or systemic change. Compassion brings possibility for differentiated leadership. *Compassion is the ability to feel with and then take action in ways serving the person's and system's greater good.* Compassion, unlike empathy or even sympathy, takes action. A compassionate leader can certainly understand the impact life circumstances have on an employee and still decide not to renew a contract. Such a leader also knows that changing the rules of a game while the game is being played rarely leads to positive results.

Rather than empathy, choose compassion and responsibility. When leaders focus on responsibility—i.e., they function for themselves and lead a system to function optimally—emotional reactions are easily exposed as futile attempts to derail processes of change. Responsibility—to be "response-able"—is a key trait of differentiated leadership and systems. Where attention to responsibility fails, where persons are not held accountable for the roles and functions that would be inherent to their job descriptions, where mistakes made and poor functioning and reasoning are overlooked, even excused, one can expect continuous disruption to the emotional process seeking change. Time and energy will be sucked from the system, getting more and more people reactive, leaving the system with less than all the members within the system would suggest. In larger systems, this can lead to totalitarian leadership. In healthy systems one finds the system is bigger than the sum of all its parts.

Differentiated leaders embrace compassion and accountability

Poorly differentiated leaders lacking responsibility expose themselves in many ways. One we as authors detest is the meeting without agenda materials distributed in advance. Colleagues show up, some a few minutes late, not knowing what to expect, other than expecting to report in the meeting. The chair then typically states it should be a short meeting as there is not much to discuss. Those who do report find little engagement from others on what was shared. Inevitably, someone will raise an issue taking the meeting on a wild goose chase, often an issue that has been batted back and forth many times, even over years. This "new" issue—never imagined by the agenda or the chair—now takes more time than what was allocated for the meeting. The meeting ends with unresolved matters and members being tasked to prepare material around the issue raised for the next meeting. With the time filled, the chair feels it was a productive meeting. Those differentiated from the system know it was an utter waste of time. Systems rarely reckon such a waste of time for they know it will reflect a significant loss of potential, time, and finances.

Of course, it is not only unproductive meetings that reveal the lack of responsibility in leadership and systems. Conversations and discernment around gender, race, class, ability, religion, and other intersectional themes often succumb to the power of empathy and the lack of responsibility. Whether it is the media or culture more broadly, emotional arguments are used to coax and dissuade persons along narrow ideological lines. The unjust and painful history of Western society has with these matters, is left untouched. The staff may reflect diversity, but the system never changed to function at a higher level of differentiation, which inevitably includes higher levels of ethical discernment. Performance reviews and budgets are equally susceptible to emotional manipulation. Leaders would prefer to avoid the conflict inherent in a poor review, to resist the sense of loss of not renewing a contract, and to see a well-liked employee go. Friedman reminds us that failed responsibility leads to systems that flounder, even die. *Where have you seen the lack of responsibility being tolerated, even celebrated? How would you lead differently? How do you rank your sense of responsibility as a person, a partner, a parent, and a professional?*

Claiming Responsibility

The survival and flourishing of an organization are co-determined by responsibility, especially as unforeseen events impact the system. Differentiated systems that function optimally forward leaders who embrace their optimal functioning and who can remain less anxious in crisis moments. Leaders who cannot stay connected to persons in times of anxiety will disappoint themselves and fail in their charge. Most leaders learned early in life to take emotional, relational, and even financial responsibility for themselves or family members as parental and societal forms of care failed. Imagine a child stepping in where an alcoholic parent neglects family care, or one sibling protecting others against abuse by assuring their siblings will not draw unwanted attention and get in "trouble" with a parent. Where someone assumes responsibility for members in their system, their overfunctioning outward often reveals underfunctioning in the system, i.e., they are not taking responsibility for their own well-being. Certainly, in a situation where a loved one is differently abled and in need of care, the care provided shows love and compassion, but that love cannot replace the need for each family member, also the one with special needs, to claim responsibility for their own life, to self-differentiate within their system.

Responsibility ultimately speaks to one's ability to self-regulate. Mindfulness of one's reactive tendencies will kick-start self-regulation. So too seeking out mentors and persons more differentiated than you are. If you do not know such a person, you can ask around and seek empowerment from a consultant, coach, or even therapist. Consistently, dialogue with one's inner critic, always loud in the undifferentiated, is needed. Imagining oneself as a differentiated leader will bring a variety of responses one can evaluate. Should the situation be extremely difficult, self-compassion for being at the center of the difficulty will curb reactivity. Since tension-filled moments often derail paying attention to one's personal, relational, and familial goals, return to those alongside your professional aspirations. One can always better self-regulate if one becomes a member of another system that functions more optimally. Sports teams, clubs, spiritual practices, and even religious affiliations can buffer against a toxic system. Without accepting responsibility for one's presence in a system, a leader will not only fail at self-differentiation, they will also remain highly reactive to situations while showing little mindfulness they are part of bigger systems. Unhealthy organisms—viruses and cancer cells are examples—multiply and even flourish unaware they are part of another organism, which is now diseased.

Working toward the greater good demands responsibility. This raises significant questions and concerns for families who allow abuse, addiction, and troubling family members to undermine everyone's well-being or a system such as the United States where fiscal responsibility remains elusive for the government and many individuals alike. *What might a significant lack of responsibility say about the leaders America chooses?* Of course, the same dynamics around responsibility unfold in all organizations, whether for profit or not.

Responsibility demands a keen awareness of the other, whether they are individuals, groups, communities, or even nature. Reactive leaders focus on select stakeholders only and believe the system will adapt to their vision (or needs), for their vision is the only correct one. They tend to focus on the procedure—even rituals—beginning a meeting with meditation or prayer—without an awareness of how the emotional process receives such rituals. When some members react, often grouped due to togetherness forces, reactive leaders join those groups in groupthink. It is warped irony that reactive leaders often receive large bonuses whereas their fellow employees barely receive cost-of-living increases or worse, are let go due to financial exigencies. Where responsibility is lacking, dysfunction, crisis, and chaos increase. As those forces grow exponentially, persons and systems wane.

To make things worse, leaders who lack a sense of responsibility for their emotional process do not know when or how to step out of their roles or leadership position. Their anxiety propels them to stay in the game when the game has long since changed or left them behind. This anxiety coincides with a fear, possibly unacknowledged, that the only identity they know, being a leader, is propping up a weak self. With self-protecting illusion, poorly differentiated leaders believe the system will fail without them, and they are irreplaceable. Serving their weak egos, some leaders seek purposeless immortality, initiating new strategic plans just as they step out and forcing the next leader to follow the plan for the next number of years. Of course, behind this fear is the kernel of an awareness that a more differentiated leader may step forward, exposing the poor leadership of the undifferentiated leader.

Systems that fail to differentiate or accept responsibility mirror the leaders they choose. They tend to invade the spaces of others, but since they do not develop their sense of self, their efforts to intervene falter. We recognize these dynamics especially in the United States, China, and Russia, despite having very different governmental systems. Leaders in these systems fuel anxiety, often by becoming controlling and through hostile actions. Poorly differentiated institutions and systems may get larger, but they do not grow in being more effective in reaching their own goals.

Excellent leaders are open to the future

Open to the Future

Without accepting responsibility and being able to respond
("response-able"), the future never unfolds in expected ways
even as surprise can thwart plans. Those who survived the
Nazi Holocaust taught us one's future can be "dumb luck,"
as Friedman called it.[7] Those Jews pulled into gas chambers
died. One's future is also determined by physical reality. The
farmer depending on rain sees a failed crop when drought
sets in. Self-differentiation among the farmers will not save
the crop, though it will assist them to manage the crisis and
create a new future. Nazi prisoners who were doctors and
engineers built the Autobahn by day, but at night, they built
an X-ray machine, stealing and bribing their way to do so,
and assisted their fellow prisoners with their ingenuity. One's
future is changed by being responsive to one's reality, even
if it is being in a prisoner camp. Holocaust survivor and
neurologist Victor Frankl taught us some prisoners in death
camps such as Auschwitz, where he was a prisoner and saw
his mother and brother die, do better than others if they have
meaning and purpose—having personal goals and direction.
When a person works toward personal goals—even if the goal
is staying alive while facing starvation—resiliency, persistence,
hope, and self-regulation are strengthened, while anxiety
decreases.

A differentiated leader is open to the future, knowing very
well that one cannot control others or the future. Poorly differentiated leaders not only have a firm view of what the future
looks like, but they will also force their way in a futile attempt
to realize that vision. They not only forget every action has a
reaction, that the harder they push the bigger the resistance
will be, but they also do not reckon systemic sabotage as
the homeostatic principle within an emotional process resists
change.

Notes

1. Friedman, *A Failure of Nerve: Leadership in the Age of the Quick Fix*, 202; Steinke, 8.
2. Friedman, *A Failure of Nerve: Leadership in the Age of the Quick Fix*, 132.
3. Ibid.
4. Ibid., 133.
5. Ibid., 137.
6. Ibid.
7. Ibid., 154.

TRANSFORMING SYSTEMS

Chapter 5

Driving Change: Putting Theory into Practice

Effective leaders lead, and people and systems are transformed. Poor leadership also leads to change, but often not a successful change. Self-differentiated leaders understand bringing change demands transforming the emotional process. Some are tasked to bring change and others discover broken systems and processes needing to be addressed. No doubt you've discovered the challenges of growing and transforming a system. Inevitably, any attempt to bring change will be met with resistance equal in intensity to the change that needs to be implemented. Remaining less anxious is paramount, as is having the awareness one seeks to change the very system one is a member of.

Self-differentiation, as you have discerned reading thus far into the book, is foundational to leadership. Still, self-differentiation is not all that is needed for effective leadership. In this third part of the book, we offer a few techniques to assist you in facilitating forward-thinking and transformation in your organization. The techniques will be very difficult, if not impossible to facilitate should you underfunction and not pay

DOI: 10.4324/9781003463993-9

attention to your emotional processes, at home and at work. We imagine you being empowered to lead with less anxiety and more confidence.

When Sir Isaac Newton saw the apple fall from the tree, he surmised there was a great force at work: *gravity*. It would have been easy for him to assume the tree had tired of holding on to the apple and had decided to let go. Because Newton looked beyond the obvious, he gave us a deeper understanding of gravity and the fundamental laws of motion, namely:

- A stationary body or one in constant motion will stay stationary or on the designated path unless acted upon by a force.
- How fast a body or entity accelerates will depend on its mass and how much force is applied to it.
- For every action there is an equal and opposite reaction (see Table 5.4 below).

All change needs some force to overcome resistance

We have all experienced organizational resistance. This is Newton's third law—for every action there is an equal and opposite reaction—a reality that frustrates all leaders. When we move an organization to change, the members and its processes apply an oppositional force equal to all attempts to bring change. As if having a mind of its own, the organization pushes back and resists change.

As a leader, when you are trying to change an organization, you need to apply a force to realize the goals and purposes serving its vision and mission. The faster you want your organization to change, the more you want to accelerate toward the new performance outputs or vision, the greater the force you need to apply. The larger the organization, the greater the force you need to apply to get it to change. In organizational terms we would not use a term like force, but we would use terms like critical mass, scaling the change, over communicating the change needed, these are all forms of force in Newton's definition.

Organizations get comfortable, the boiling frog apologue, and will cruise along in a given direction until someone comes along and seeks to initiate change. This is Newton's first law. Organizations will not change unless an external force is applied to them. Their natural state is to be a boiling frog.

A self-differentiated leader recognizes the natural state of the organization and the people and processes that make up the organization. Thinking about the organization along Newton's law of motion allows the leader to acknowledge that the current state of things is not so much a flaw or a defect that should be criticized but a realty of how systems mature and work.

To be a good and effective leader it is obviously critical then that you understand and can articulate why a change is needed. You will meet resistance, even with a clear rational for change: *Why change, especially if business and profits are good? Why not just keep on moving in the same direction as before?*

Despite a world of constant change and unpredictability, Newton's first law of motion, as well as the systems concept of homeostasis (see Chapter 2), keep people happily going about their daily routines. These folk are in constant motion but experience little evident change. Since systems repeat themselves, we can almost predict the outcome as no or little change.

Newton's second law is obvious: If you want to change the direction of a very large body, organization, or even a country, and you want to do it quickly, then you'll need a very large force. Many countries have used an invasion or a *coup d'état* to bring about instant change. Companies may experience a *coup d'état* of sorts—a hostile takeover. Less aggressive approaches are mergers or partnerships. Regardless of their form, such shifts often involve large-scale changes at the top of the organization and require significant funding and consulting support to complete.

How will you structure and implement the force needed to bring change to your institution? On whose support will you draw to facilitate change? What will you do if your attempt to initiate change brings unintended consequences, for systems rarely act entirely predictably in response to change? The leadership implications around change remain complex even as systems theory allows us to gain deeper insights.

The third law—the most overlooked—states for every action there is an equal and opposite reaction. The previous chapters highlighted systemic reactions to anxiety or tension caused by any attempt to bring change. Imagine yourself as a leader during a hostile takeover. *What reactions do you anticipate in both organizations? Who is most likely to sabotage the process? How will you lead one institution to take over another?* Or imagine being the leader of a smaller institution in a merger, knowing very well the new institution formed does not need two executives. *How will you participate in the necessary discussions as you imagine yourself possibly seeking new employment soon? How will you remain present in the conversation? How will you respond to employees' inevitable frustration, uncertainty, anger, and general animosity the change precipitates?* Consistently, it will be the levels of self-differentiation within both systems and their members determining much of the process.

Change demands addressing resistance

Sometimes we get wrapped up in the belief our vision, mission, and actions are sufficient to deliver change. "Why would anyone push back or react?," we wonder as we forget about sabotage and resistance. Yes, anxious people afraid of change will sabotage the new process, leadership team, or organization, regardless of how good you think the transformation is and is being communicated. Indeed, so common is sabotage that Friedman warns "the capacity of a leader to be prepared for, to be aware of, and to learn how to deal skillfully with this type of crisis [namely sabotage] may be the most important aspect of leadership. It is the key to the kingdom."[1]

Anxiety, resistance, and sabotage have real-world implications. It is estimated a whopping 70% of change initiatives fail.[2] And even those attempts that succeed show that 66% of cases end with undesired outcomes.[3] Not surprisingly, workforce productivity declines 57% during periods of transition.[4] The cost of change is rarely reckoned and addressing sabotage and the anxiety in the emotional process holds much potential.

Why does institutional change have such a dismal record? Besides systemic reactions going unaddressed, leadership complacency can be named. Business consultant John Kotter in his book *Leading Change* identifies various reasons for complacency, including too much "happy talk" from senior leaders, internal measurement systems focusing on the wrong performance indexes, low overall performance standards, lack of performance feedback, a kill-the-messenger culture, and the human capacity for denial.[5] Many examples can be given of a corporation that resisted change. One stands out: *Kodak*.

Eastman Kodak Company, or *Kodak* as it is more commonly known, is a good example of just how difficult it is to change a large organization. *Kodak* was a brand once as recognizable as *Apple* or *Google* is today. From humble beginnings in 1880, it peaked in 1996 with 145,000 employees and two-thirds of the global film market. Most people reading *The Essence of Leadership* will either remember the transition from film to digital photography or will only know the latter. *Kodak* currently focuses on niche film businesses and other imaging technologies after near failure. The company came out of Chapter 11 bankruptcy court in 2013 and now has a mere 4,500 employees.[6] Let's give *Kodak* some credit: the company survived when many institutions did not, even in a reimagined form. So despite being a change poster child, much maligned and studied, *Kodak* remains a company showing profits, a testament to the leadership team who continue to initiate change when others might have left or sold the company.

If the natural state of an organization is to keep moving in the same direction and to resist change, then it makes sense that changing direction is hard, both to facilitate and to experience.

Being able to implement change successfully is a key skill for every leader. In this chapter, we will share a change process that leaders can follow and use with their leadership team and organization to increase the probability of success. The process is captured by the following acronym **DRIVERS**, which represents key elements interwoven with the emotional process you need to have in place when you embark on a change plan (see Figure 5.1). DRIVERS stands for

- **D**issatisfaction
- **R**ecruiting critical mass
- **I**nitial step(s)
- **V**ision
- **E**thics
- **R**esistance
- **S**ponsor.

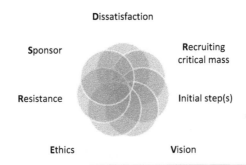

Figure 5.1   The DRIVERS of change.

DRIVERS is rooted in the theory of change. When leaders focus on only one element, say *Vision*, or they think one element of the change plan is more important than the others, say, overcoming or removing *Resistance*, they are more likely to fail. Embracing *every* component of DRIVERS will empower you to facilitate change in your system, regardless of how desperate or self-satisfied your system might be. It will open new possibilities for your leadership. Skilled leaders quickly assess and create an inventory of which DRIVERS elements are either missing or in most need of boosting in their organization. They recognize that change management, like strategy, is not linear and cannot be fully represented by formulas. DRIVERS is best visualized as interconnected circles, spiraling into each other, each element taking the lead for a brief while to step back and see another element leading.

Change can be initiated from any part of the system

DRIVERS: A Brief Introduction

Before we discuss how the elements of DRIVERS propel change, let's unpack the acronym.

D: Dissatisfaction

Without dissatisfaction with the present state of things, change will remain elusive. As a leader, you can create dissatisfaction by highlighting what is "wrong" or broken in a system. The leadership task is clear: Create discomfort with the status quo. Add anxiety to the system. Excellent leaders can highlight complacency or failing processes, even underfunctioning or overfunctioning teams; they call forth new ways of being and doing, and get folks out of their comfort zones. They communicate workplace complacency or that the status quo is not going to remain the norm. Undifferentiated leaders will seek ways to resolve the tension rather than inducing tension and remaining less anxious in the tension field. Managed dissatisfaction invites more anxiety into the system and its members, even a system already straining under anxiety. Tension is an important catalyst for change. This is Newton's first law, making people uncomfortable with the current path they are following.

R: Recruit Critical Mass

Corporate and systemic change requires a critical mass of persons to embrace a new way of being and doing. As a leader, you cannot implement change on your own. Instead, you will need to recruit people who believe in the vision you're offering, and the change for which you're asking; persons who will follow your lead. Think of this as the small group going to apply the force to move the system in a different direction. The scale of change you seek will determine how large this critical mass—the group around you, including all levels of employees—needs to be. An optimal group is more differentiated than the rest of the organization. This is Newton's second law, building the amount of force you will need to get the organization to change direction: Big change, big critical mass, small change, small critical mass.

I: Initial Step(s)

The first or initial step is important and can be difficult to conceive. Since change can be overwhelming, offering those you lead a practical first step in support of the new Vision creates the impetus for further change. The first step is often simply to work collaboratively with your small group to discern the change needed.

V: Vision

Vision demands you and your team provide a clear picture of the future. This includes imagining the intended and unintended consequences of the steps you are about to take. Make your blind faith visible.

E: Ethical

A leader's belief in their ability to bring about change— a strong narcissistic trait—can confuse ethical boundaries. Often there is a fine line between brilliance and insanity, and genius and irrationality. Ethics demands clear values, transparency, and a constant awareness of relational and professional covenants.

R: Remove Resistance

Since there is no change without resistance, overcoming resistance and sabotage are primary leadership tasks (see Chapter 3). Any attempt to bring change with no systemic reaction is not change deep enough to touch the emotional process and is likely to fail. Remember Newton's third law—for every action there is an equal and opposite action (see Table 5.4 below). It is more effective to address and eliminate the resisting force, the reaction, than it is to keep applying action. This effectively leads to an arms race and people become grid locked at loggerheads. When leaders do not actively work on removing resistance the outcome is often better known as a "go-slow," quiet quitting, or a strike.

S: Sponsor

Leaders seeking change should expect hitting walls and feeling the weight of the task at hand. Seeking mentors and self-differentiated conversation partners in anxious times adds the possibility to a leader's desire to initiate and maintain the change. This is all the more important for cultivating sustainable change signing up for a marathon, not a sprint. Sponsors provide a good sounding board and insights are often missed when you are in the grip of change. Make sure you have people you trust you can turn to when the going gets tough.

Icon Co.: A Company in Need of Change

Icon Co. was created by combining a traditional photographic film business with a new digital video print and media storage business. It is a business unit of a much larger corporation, *Chemical Co.* In the early 1990s, the generally accepted view was consumers would use digital cameras and then print their photos at home using a digital video printer. *Icon Co.* had partnered with one of the major Japanese camera manufacturers to make the film for their cameras. They had also invested heavily in the future of that manufacturer. *Icon Co.* built manufacturing capacity and recruited heavily to meet this future demand. They had ambitious revenue growth projections that were needed to cover a cost base building on their assumption of a large global consumer market.

The mismatch in revenue and expenses resulted in significant operating losses. The losses were projected to turn into profits as revenues started to increase exponentially from consumers printing their photos at home. *Icon Co.* also increased employees from a few hundred to about a thousand. Just as production was established and the digital photo print material was available for shipment to the retailer and the consumer, the Japanese manufacturer concluded that there would not be a global market for home photo print material after all. *Icon Co.* had the wrong vision and pursued the wrong path, placing them in a precarious position.

The digital print market was now limited to the small and diverse novelty industry, demanding numerous applications and printer types. Amusement rides and tourist spots are some of these markets; rollercoaster patrons are enticed to purchase a photo of themselves on the ride or tourists can purchase a photo without any wait. With arms raised, hair standing on end, faces screaming, bodies dripping wet, and having a great time, a photo captures the essence of their holiday. Photo booths, photo transfer to mugs, and other novelty gifts in which photos play a role were also markets in which *Icon Co.* could sell print media. There were industrial applications for the technology, most noteworthy among them being security cards and passports. Digital technology offered increased security, enhanced counterfeit protection, and greater flexibility to store and share images with security agencies.

Despite the excitement of these new markets and technologies, *Icon Co.* still needed to address a traditional film manufacturing business that was in rapid decline. The leadership now faced several challenges. It had aging assets and the window of opportunity for selling to traditional markets was closing. The anticipated mass consumer market opportunity never materialized. The remaining niche markets were small and fragmented, and *Icon Co.* was not positioned to serve such markets. It had organized itself to be a supplier to original equipment manufacturers and was not an aftermarket supplier. No surprise the company's cost structure exceeded revenues as *Icon Co.* burned through its cash reserves. *Icon Co.* had gone from being a small business operating below the radar at *Chemical Co.* for almost 30 years, to now being a very visible cash drain and in much need of attention.

The original vision of a mass consumer market, printing at home, had been very compelling. Consumers bought home PCs and started using inkjet printers to print various documents, including color documents. Why not photographs? *Icon Co.*'s leaders argued. Yet it was difficult to argue against the market analysis, investment, and commitment of their Japanese partner. Rather than focusing on what had gone wrong with the market analysis, there was now a pressing need to address the future of *Icon Co.* With limited revenue growth opportunities and an oversized cost base, there was a dire need to restructure.

Icon Co. has taken a bold step by combining traditional and new technologies in one location. The concept was to create a new vibrant business built on the foundation of traditional photographic film technology. As the new technologies replaced the old, the business would continue to evolve and expand, the company thought. There had been challenges with this integration. With bold promises of investments, new jobs, and expansive global markets, the new and old had found their peace with the changes that had already started to take place. Expansion and growth cure many evils and alleviate many concerns.

When the reality that major change was going to be needed started to sink in, the lines were drawn in the sand. The traditional businesses within *Chemical Co.* were clear about who should bear the brunt of the blame for the financial situation and distanced themselves from a new digital future. Although those in the new digital business unit understood this failure, rather than abandon all this new technology they were more inclined to regroup and try a different approach.

Hoping to avoid legacy issues or bias about the right path to pursue in the future, *Chemical Co.* started by appointing new leaders for *Icon Co.* These leaders then set about recruiting their critical mass for change. *Icon Co.* trained the new leaders in DRIVERS and tasked them with delivering change.

Leading toward Change

DRIVERS can give the impression change is linear, a step-by-step process. As pictured in this chapter, we imagine a spiraling, dynamic process. Fundamentally, the dynamics defining DRIVERS are paradoxical in nature. Each driver is crucial to change (as we'll discuss next by looking at *Dissatisfaction*), but no driver holds the exclusive key to effective change. This both/and nature requires intuitive leadership. *What comes first: Dissatisfaction or Vision? What is more important, a differentiated leader or having a clear strategy for change? How can recruitment overcome resistance?* The answers to questions like these inevitably expose the gray, complex nature of leadership and change. Still, DRIVERS can empower you to grow your confidence and skill.

D: Dissatisfaction: Finding Fault with the Status Quo

Both systems theory's homeostatic principle and Newton's first law state people will continue on their current path unless someone applies a force interrupting that path. Like most things in life, we seldom change voluntarily. Far more likely is a crisis or traumatic event propelling us to change. Cardiac arrests or being diagnosed with diabetes are good examples of a jolt or a force prompting people to change their life habits. For years those now facing a significant health scare continued on a path that led them to the crisis. Prior knowledge or insight did not initiate change: the crisis did. Few people will change if they see no reason to do so. You now know good reasons why persons and systems, with their emotional processes, resist change. Who then is volunteering to upset a peaceful, predictable life to deal with change? Your task as a leader is to sow dissatisfaction with the present state; to introduce anxiety or tension to a system, and to disrupt people's comfort zones.

Deliberately creating dissatisfaction is something that creates discomfort in leaders. There is a sense they are manipulating the situation to achieve their objective. However, creating dissatisfaction does not have to be manipulative. You can focus on needed changes that are genuine and appropriate. By highlighting dissatisfaction, you also show the cost of not changing. Dissatisfaction creates the anxiety needed to get people to see the futility of current practices. Creating change demands feeling when others want you to think, and vice versa, or that you hold a different opinion when others want you to agree. Even entering into tension-filled conversations when others would prefer to keep the peace can be the catalyst for change.

There are many additional ways to cause and highlight dissatisfaction. One sure way is to be more transparent about finances. *Who gets paid what? Do the executives receive bonuses when the institution is running at a loss? Are men paid more than women or are there differences across color lines? Can the institution pay its bills and make payroll?* Few things get people as focused as talking about money. Another easy starting point for creating dissatisfaction with the current state is to look for areas of excess and eliminate those. If some people are getting perks, such as preferred parking spaces, remove them. Establish the principle that getting to work early—not your title—earns you the right to get the first parking spot. Privileged seating in the dining room or even separate dining rooms implies some people are more important than others. Eliminate this. If tables are oblong, replace them with round tables, and in so doing encourage people to engage and work as teams, even at lunch.

A third way to show dissatisfaction is to communicate what is happening in the industry or to similar institutions. Use examples of companies who resisted change and point out what happened to them. Paint a vivid picture of a doom scenario. You can also bring in customers and have them explain to your executive leadership or team what is going on in the market, why they are changing, and why they need you to change in response.

A fourth sure way to create energy around dissatisfaction is to expose individuals who are underperforming and remove them from your workforce. Hold people accountable and increase responsibility across all levels of the organization. Establish the principle of a minimum standard of performance. Terminate anyone below this standard. Do not hesitate to tie pay increases to performance and outcomes—reaching predetermined goals—rather than just a standard increase across the board. Winning is a habit. So start creating winning habits.

A fifth way, already alluded to in the previous four suggestions, is to focus more on *the way things are* than on *the way they should be*. This seems counterintuitive, but denying the lived experience of people and an institution comes at a steep cost. Employees aren't fools. Nurses and doctors, for example, may discern *the way it is*, is they have limited time to be with clients or patients. *The way it should be* is that the patient or customer comes first. *The way it is,* is the company not on a sustainable financial path. *The way it should be* the company should flourish as an organization, also financially. *The way it is—there are* very different ideas about how to address the current situation. *The way it should be*—all need to agree on how to proceed. *The way it is*—the team is wandering in a desert. *The way it should be*—the team should enter the promised land of milk and honey; and so on.

Exploring the way things are now is the essential work a leader needs to do. Asking a team or coworkers how they experience unfolding events is not being a therapist. It is being a compassionate, *significant leader. Significant leaders*, when they explore *the way it is*, might experience a short increase in anxiety as the system reacts to years of poor process, keeping secrets, avoidances, and stonewalling (indicating concerns but not addressing them).[7] Instead, the anxiety will be replaced with healthy tension and anticipation, which are neither toxic nor something to be avoided. *Dominant leaders*, chasing *the way it should be* without recognizing the way it is, inevitably increases the anxiety in a system (see Figure 5.2). These leaders will force their way and will over people. Anxious systems not only are on the path to failure, but they also will invent other anxieties through a process of selective exclusion: they tend to avoid the real issues and pursue secondary or minor issues, often vigorously.

Whereas exploring *the way it is* can be eye-opening, dominant leaders often present illusory visions to distract, detract, or even deny reality. Politicians especially are masters of dominant, illusory leadership. How they have come to believe illusions will prevail remains a mystery since no powerful empire has succeeded to survive over time. Illusions are powerful. *Who on your team will help you discover what your team, your institution, or your industry is experiencing? Who will help you navigate matters of intersectionality, i.e., how power permeates and influences gender, sexual orientation, race, class, ethnicity, age, religion, and ability; how data are processed? How will others recognize you as a significant leader, not someone seeking to dominate?*

Though illusions can be the screen onto which a leader projects control and competence, emperors without clothes are always exposed. And though some people will hold on to an illusion as their hoped-for reality, one cannot wish a reality into existence. Here *illusion* remains true to its etymological roots, from the Latin *illūdō*, to be mocked or ridiculed. Leaders who cannot engage reality as *the way it is* will be exposed as incompetent.

Looking at *the way it is*, which removes the blinders of denial, keeps a leader from fleeing reality. Invite persons to complain about their work experience or criticize the institution (and especially the administration), for in those comments is hidden the impetus for change. Not all leaders—especially those who lean toward narcissism, who want to be liked, and who are poorly differentiated—can stomach the difficult conversations envisioned here. We'll return to significant leadership below.

Dominant leaders increase the anxiety in their system by focusing on *the way it should be*. Should the anxiety rise too high, the system will retract and resist all change. Significant leaders, when they focus on *the way it is*, not only lower the gap existing between *the way it is* and *the way it should be*, but they also keep anxiety at a level where anxiety supports change.

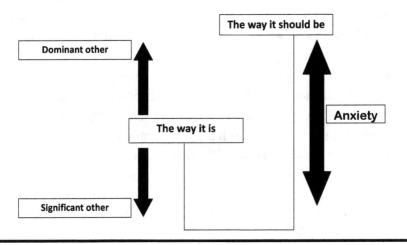

Figure 5.2   Significant leadership and "the way it is."

Dissatisfaction has to be a conscious effort. If you do not have an approach to create discomfort, you are back to pushing the vision and hoping for self-enlightenment or self-initiated change to take place. Moving forward by these means is highly unlikely. Rather, as a leader, you have entered the realm of wishful thinking and are juggling illusory balls. We better heed General Colin Powell's first lesson in his *Leadership Primer*: "Being responsible sometimes means pissing people off."[8] Powell reminds us good leadership accepts responsibility for the group as a whole, which inevitably means some individuals will be or will feel left out. Leaders who are unable to face criticism, engage in conflict, and yes, even know they are not appreciated or liked, will become stuck in the status quo. Continue to work on your self-differentiation and remain less anxious.

R: *Recruiting a Critical Mass: Gathering People Ready for Change*

Recruiting critical mass does not necessarily mean recruiting *new* people. The first step is to see who in the current organization can be "recruited" for the change plan. The critical mass will exclude those who are supportive but remain passive, those seeking change but according to a different vision, and those who will oppose or sabotage the change efforts. Every team, organization, and boardroom exhibits these different, often unspoken engagement behaviors. Differences in opinions and engagement often lead to splinter groups forming within larger groups. People "buddy up" or enmesh based on common values, goals, or concerns. "Misery loves company," we say. As folk enmesh around similar group thinking, they undermine the change program, particularly if they are going to oppose the change.

The leadership team needs to be disciplined in working through the engagement levels systematically and aligning everyone for a change. Document a specific plan for each person in this realignment process, a plan that is clear about the role and function a person will play in the change process. Clear expectations promote and elicit accountability.

There need not be consensus around the change needed

A common error leaders make is to assume everyone must agree with the change. Often all you need is for people not to oppose you or sabotage the process. In most cases, this will be more than sufficient for successful change. If certain groups or individuals acquiesce to the pending change process, that is often enough to allow the organization to move forward. This was the reality *Icon Co.* faced:

> *Icon Co.* needed to reduce the workforce by 50 percent to bring the cost structure more in line with revenues. The company needed to manage this reduction by selecting the most appropriate people for the positions it needed going forward. This selective employment approach would need to be extended to the unionized labor force. Labor unions typically prefer a last in first out (LIFO) approach.

> The leadership believed the future of *Icon Co.* required a blend of skills and knowledge, which many of the new people who had recently been added to the workforce had. Relying just on historical experience with the company seemed inconsistent with the vision for the future. Rather than asking the unions to agree with this stance, which would

have violated their core principles and practice, the leadership engaged with all the union members and area officials to explain why LIFO would produce a suboptimal working organization. LIFO would not guarantee that the employees had the skills needed for the future. The leadership developed a selection process that included service as one element of five components. The other four components were based on line management review, technical test batteries such as engineering, mathematics, special awareness, and behavioral event interviewing. The approach would be to select the most appropriate people for the future organizational structure. The leadership took the union representatives through mock tests to demonstrate this process was not going to disadvantage experience.

At no point then did the leadership compromise the principles and ethics of good union representation. They never asked the unions to agree with the plan, but to understand the merits of it and not to resist the change or enter a strike.

The union leadership recognized going through a selective employment process might be worth it for the company's long-term success. Going on strike could have been a more typical response, an act that would have caused everyone suffering. Part of what made this alternative way of moving forward acceptable to the unions was the ethical way the leadership approached how to reduce the workforce. (See the discussion of *Ethics* below).

The numbers reduction was achieved without any disruptive action by the unions, who stayed fully engaged and were good monitors of the process to ensure it was done fairly. The leadership set up redeployment resources that provided generous support to those that lost their jobs. A key distinction in the change process was to move people out of jobs and not immediately terminate employment. The first step was to explain their job had come to an end, but their employment would continue from the redeployment office. Their new job was to find a new job. Employees were given a fixed amount of time to work with the redeployment office to find themselves new jobs. This was extremely successful and very few, if any individuals were terminated, almost all found new jobs within the time frame they were given. Clearly this leadership team was part of the newly formed critical mass.

When a leader acts toward change, strange things start to happen. We discussed in Chapter 2 the systemic reactions you can expect in such a situation. People may behave differently, even "badly." Suddenly, conflict and generalized hostility can increase. Gossip and skepticism may appear and undermine the process. Some employees may even argue the leadership is tackling the wrong issue or the right issue in the wrong way. Therefore it is important the leadership team understands what is going on in the emotional process and be the less anxious entity in the reactive system. As leaders get all involved in the change at the appropriate engagement level, their chances of success start to increase exponentially.

It isn't necessary or even preferable to have every supervisor or leader making challenging decisions reverberating the system. The higher the number of perceived leaders, the more challenging it is to keep communication lines clear and hold on to a common vision. Rather, with many cooks in the kitchen, one can expect poor communication, blurred authority lines, and decision-making processes derailed. The idea is to move leaders to a supportive engagement level, to be more of a sponsor (see below) than a driver of change. When the most senior level executive—possibly the one who initiated the need for change in the first place—remains involved in the minutiae of the change process, micro-managing it, they will become bogged down. Discern with your leadership team the level of engagement required of each person to see the change process through to success.

It is important to identify all the major players in the organization and where they are positioned in the system. Once the team maps out where the current engagement level is it needs to decide where these individuals' engagement level optimally should sit. An action plan is then needed to create each move. This is a bit like positioning players on a chess board or football field. You can consider four types of engagement: Support, Drive (change), Engaged/Active, and Oppose.

Where a leader in a specific role (marketing, for example) resists the change, develop a plan to change their orientation to "Drive", or change the VP of marketing (see Table 5.1). Should another leader be over-involved in the dynamics of change, trying to drive the change themselves without collaboration and collegiality, move them to the "Support" role. Invite a third leader to drive discussions with employees. Here we imagine a midsize organization with several leaders in various roles:

Recruit Critical Mass

Table 5.1 Mapping Out Engagement Levels to Establish Critical Mass

Force field analysis	Support	Drive	Engaged	Oppose	Action
Executive Chair	O	X			In this case, the executive chair is too involved in the change—move them to sponsor/support mode.
Head of Research			O	X	Split research into two operations; do not let the Head of Research limit new technologies.
VP of Operations		O	X		VP will need to be one of the key proponents for change; this team member needs to be involved—or replaced if the person cannot drive change.
Chief Financial Officer		O	X		The business must explore all financial options and stop cash outflows; sell assets and joint ventures; reduce the workforce as needed. Thus the CFO has to lean in and has a central role to play.
Marketing Director		X	O		The Marketing Director needs to shift focus to the external world and support customers and new markets. Prevent this position from becoming over-involved in the internal organizational change plan.

(Continued)

Table 5.1 (Continued) Mapping Out Engagement Levels to Establish Critical Mass

Force field analysis	Support	Drive	Engaged	Oppose	Action
HR Director		O⟶		X	HR needs to be part of Critical Mass. Replace the HR Director if the person is resisting the required change. This might be a difficult decision and could apply to any role where you have to move someone from the Oppose Box. It is wise to move someone from Oppose to Drive. There might be roles that are not critical to success and so long as the person does not continue to oppose/resist the change you can tolerate them being in the organization.

Larger organizations need more critical mass. Co-workers need not fully support the change sought, but they also mustn't be allowed to sabotage the leadership. Getting persons to acquiesce is often easier than convincing persons to agree with the new vision. Discerning the level of engagement of each leadership line is important, but engaging opposition often consumes most of a leader's time. We will discuss this more under "Removing Resistance." Here, suffice to say, people who are actively engaged in opposing the change need to be dealt with quickly and effectively.

As you start to align the engagement across and through the organization, you start to create a critical mass sufficiently large to implement the necessary changes. This critical mass, importantly, is aligned with your vision and there are no or fewer forces working against you.

Communications theorist and sociologist Everett Rogers in his book, *Diffusion of Innovations*, reminds us there will be no critical mass unless you reach the minds of the workforce, not just the leadership.[9] At some point, you need to win enough hearts and minds to make the change sustainable; the critical mass can get things going. To move the entire organization you must find the early adopters, those who are first to come on board, and the flexible majority, those who will readily follow your leadership, to support you. These secondary groups are critical in gaining momentum and in carrying the organization forward. Use your leadership team to target these groups.

Persons who see themselves as innovators, those creative individuals who bring forth new solutions or processes after a path toward change have been determined, often frustrate a change process. Innovators will initially be excited about your change leadership and then they will get bored with it, moving on to new ideas and possibly even a new vision. Putting innovators in critical positions to facilitate change requires them to lead in ways foreign to who they are. Instead, keep them in the "lab" and in other settings where innovation is sorely needed and the process of change looks vastly different. Leaders who seek constant and fast change create unsustainable futures.

Just as you'll waste your time with innovators, you'll waste time if you try and convert the laggards, those persons who struggle to get on board with the new plan. *Since it is highly unlikely that they will change, why waste your time and energy trying to convince them to follow the process?* Do visit those who are slow to join the change process and make sure they are not actively opposing and sabotaging the process. If you discern they are a benign presence, leave them alone. Do not spend much energy on either the innovators or laggards, but do so with the early adopters and the flexible majority (see Figure 5.3).

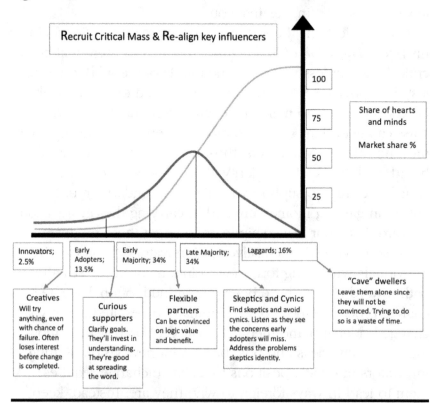

Figure 5.3   Realign persons and positions to achieve critical mass.

It is also important to seek out experienced and wise people at every level of engagement. Find healthy skeptics, not cynics, who can help you see your blind spots. At *Icon Co.* a handful of skeptics on the change leadership team had an uncanny knack for pointing out when group think—the dynamic where a group seeks to decide by discouraging creativity and individuality—was taking over and the leadership team was losing touch with reality and their core goals.

The groups we've mentioned, such as the innovators, the laggards, and the flexible majority, can be placed on this bell curve:[10]

Recruiting a critical mass of people is important as your system is inherently relational. Without relational equity— without having people on board who will follow you—your change efforts will inevitably fail. Of course, you need to discern an initial step to take to show not only your commitment to change but also to initiate movement toward a changed system.

I: Initial Step(s): Decisions with Actions Indicating Change Is Coming

Getting people to take the first step on a new path is a significant task. If you are working within a corporate culture that has been doing things a certain way for many years, changing direction can be daunting. Homeostasis shows why a certain system has become troubled even as existing employees leave or new employees join the system. A keen awareness of homeostasis can guide the creation of strategies for change and it can help in developing criteria to distinguish real change from dysfunctional reactivity. Regardless of the step(s) you take, remain watchful for anxious reactivity in the system. Prepare yourself not to be reactive to disagreements, negativism, anger, and hostility. Receive over-the-top compliments and criticisms but hold on to them lightly. Note who is more reactive than others. Their position in your organization can teach you about systemic dysfunction and how power flows through the system.

Homeostatic reactivity can be broken in many ways. Think of a spider's web. Touching any of the strands will make the entire web reverberate. Whether a hapless bug flies into the outer reaches of the web or the very center, the result is going to be the same: dinner for the spider and death for the bug. There is some grace in unsettling homeostasis with a first step that can take a variety of forms. You need not tackle the most pressing issue in your system first. Rather, we recommend your first step address "low hanging fruit," something such as parking or daycare or access to services for your employees. Once momentum has been built and you have a few noticeable successes, you can tackle larger issues such as the assessment of efficiency or transparency around finances in your institution. Family therapists would recommend one starts with the person perceived as the most disempowered one, often a child. Rather than asking the parents what is happening in the family, such therapists ask the child, who is very likely to speak truths the parents would never disclose. In your system, taking the first step with persons at the lower end of your hierarchy—including middle management and those on the perceived margins, such as the custodial staff—may be more fruitful than working with the executive leadership.

An initial step must overcome the (dysfunctional) stability of your system. Remember, the vision (see below) you're promoting is aspirational and still seems abstract and far away. People need to know what to do tomorrow that is different from their today and yesterday. Yes, the system may not be functioning optimally, but it is perfectly balanced, meaning the various aspects of the system, including its members, play well-defined roles and function in ways they do not want to give up. Of course being perfectly balanced does not mean the system is primed for change or growth or function optimally. Think of the initial step as placing your system off-balance, but doing so on purpose. This small step should be toward the new vision.

Bowen reminds us when homeostasis or equilibrium is shaken up, "emotional shock waves" go through the system.[11] Some core employees will leave or resign from their leadership positions; new crises can erupt, even ones that include unethical conduct. The creativity of a system to resist first steps is infinite. Remind yourself this is an unconscious reaction by persons who do not even know they are part of an emotional process. Claim your self-differentiation, remain less anxious, and lead people one step at a time. Resist asking for or expecting giant leaps.

The first steps might be:

- Giving administrative assistants more power to make decisions about discretionary expenditures.
- Getting employees to use your products.
- Being more vulnerable as a leader.
- Rewarding employee creativity around the new vision.
- Initiating an Employee Suggestion Scheme rewarding any suggestion that will assist the organization toward its new vision.
- Being transparent with employees about the financial situation of the company or department.
- Reconstituting the leadership team around the new vision.
- Removing old product lines from the business portfolio, perhaps ones that no longer make money but have survived for nostalgic reasons.
- Creating tangible protocols and opportunities showing employees they are important.
- Changing historical reporting relationships and processes to increase flexibility and agility.
- Initiating new measurements and goals and reporting them daily.

At one time or another, most of us have embarked on an effort to change some part of our lives. We've decided to stop smoking, start saving, drop a few pounds, or get a new job. As a rule, these sorts of changes don't occur overnight. They take time and persistence. And they tend to evolve through a multistage process. Research by psychologist James Prochaska, who developed a stage model for changing behavior, found that at any given time about only 20% of people needing to change an unhealthy behavior are prepared and ready to do so. He reminds us lasting change rarely occurs as the result of a single, ongoing decision to act. He points out change evolves from a subtle, complex, and sometimes circuitous progression—one involving thinking, hesitating, stepping forward, stumbling backward, and, quite possibly, starting all over again.[12]

Once you have initiated your first step(s), your leadership has taken a turn toward new and exciting possibilities.

V: *Vision: Concrete Aspirations beyond Wishes and Daydreaming*

The fourth element of driving change is *Vision*. Since DRIVERS as a theory of change has a paradoxical, spiral quality that should not be confused with a linear, step-by-step process, Vision may or may not be the fourth element of your change process. Still, you are probably familiar with some of the following statements: "Action without vision is just passing time; Vision without action is just daydreaming. Action and Vision can change the world" (ascribed to American futurist, Joel Arthur Barker). There is much written about Vision, Mission, Strategy, Tactics, and Goals, and as a leader you have your own definitions of each element. From a change management perspective we see these as all interchangeable in the change process. The nuance here is that you have some view of your forward mission, goal, strategy, and vision. We are less concerned about what you call it, and more concerned about you having some idea about what you are aiming for and can communicate it. You may resonate with the line: "If you don't know where you are going any road can take you there."[13]

By focusing on *Vision* we hope you will be clear about what your task as a leader is. The classic view of *Vision* is that it is a statement drafted by an institution to describe to its stakeholders what the institution's purposes are and what success would look like.

A vision statement should be aspirational or else the institution's employees will likely not find it sufficiently compelling to follow. Establishing a vision feeling like an incremental change or a marginal improvement always misses the point. The vision statement thus needs to stretch the organization and culture to aspire to do something ambitious or challenging. A vision statement can be visualized. Is it easy to imagine the vision statement and paint a clear mental image of the desired outcomes? Examples of inspirational and aspirational vision statements abound. Here we highlight a select few. *What do you "see" in these statements?*

- *Habitat for Humanity*: A world where everyone has a decent place to live.
- *Save the Children*: A world in which every child attains the right to survival, protection, development, and participation.
- *Alzheimer's Association*: A world without Alzheimer's disease.
- *Teach for America*: One day, all children in this nation will have the opportunity to attain an excellent education.
- *Microsoft* (at its founding): A computer on every desk and in every home.
- *Life is Good*: To spread the power of optimism.
- *Patagonia*: Build the best product, cause no unnecessary harm, and use business to inspire and implement solutions to the environmental crisis.
- *Honest Tea*: To create and promote great-tasting, healthy, organic beverages.

- *Universal Health Services*, Inc.: To provide superior quality healthcare services that: PATIENTS recommend to family and friends, PHYSICIANS prefer for their patients, PURCHASERS select for their clients, EMPLOYEES are proud of, and INVESTORS seek long-term returns.
- *Prezi*: To reinvent how people share knowledge, tell stories, and inspire their audiences to act.
- *TED*: Spread ideas.
- *Disney*: To make people happy.
- *Nike* (in the 1960s): Crush Adidas.
- *Tesla*: To accelerate the world's transition to sustainable energy.

Vision statements are not static and change over time. *Nike's* "Crush *Adidas*," for example, became "Just do it." Arguably *Nike's* vision in the 1960s was more of an action-oriented mission statement. Once *Nike* had surpassed *Adidas*, you can imagine the board declaring "Mission Accomplished," but it's unlikely they all declared "Vision Accomplished." Leaders need not get caught up in the difference between a vision and a mission statement. What matters is the leaders are clear about what their institution needs to do and why. They then communicate this clearly to the organization and build strategies (plans) around the vision or the mission.

Even if a vision statement remains unchanged, new strategies or action plans (with specific goals) may be necessary. One of the most frequently used goal structures is SMART goals:

Specific (simple, significant).
Measurable (meaningful, motivating).
Achievable (agreed, attainable).
Realistic and **R**elevant (resourced, results-based).
Time-limited (timely).

SMART goals have become ubiquitous in institutional management and are excellent for annual reviews. If we are considering change management goals, however, we are not huge fans of the SMART structure. When we are dealing with visions and aspirational goals and objectives that drive an organization in a new direction the SMART structure is too limiting. They are often in the form of an agreement, or negotiation, between employee and employer, or more specifically between an individual and their direct report. Since annual reviews are easily bogged down with making sure everything is fair, the tendency is to lower the bar so the individual does not fail and get a poor review. *Why would one accept an ambitious goal from one's supervisor if it might lead to a poor review?* When using SMART goals to drive change you are at risk of coming in too low.

> STRETCH goals encourage a person to be creative, innovative, and to try something ambitious

It is inconsistent to spend much time setting an aspirational vision and then constraining everyone to SMART goals. Instead, we recommend STRETCH goals, which are not included in individual annual reviews (see Table 5.2). STRETCH goals encourage an employee to be creative, and innovative, and to try something ambitious. There is no risk of failing, only in not trying. Let your subordinates and teams develop STRETCH goals and ask them to align those goals with the Vision. Empower the team to fail at reaching the STRETCH goals. This approach will keep Human Resources (a team that is always risk-averse) from your door. It will also engage the team's sense of adventure, exploration, and playfulness. Setting STRETCH goals and permitting team members to fail is a huge step toward creating an entrepreneurial and innovative culture. Work can be deeply satisfying, even fun. The SMART goal structure can hamper creativity and innovation. STRETCH goals allow you to fail more often, which leads to greater success.

Whereas SMART goals might be a management tool, STRETCH goals are a leadership tool:

Table 5.2   SMART Goals vs. STRETCH Goals

Management	Leadership
SMART goals	STRETCH goals
Specific: Coordinates—a very specific place.	**Strategic:** Begin a process and adjust as you continue.
Mensurable: Defined parameters and variables.	**Trending:** Trending over longer periods to see patterns and opportunities. Follow the trend lines, not the headlines. Don't be distracted by short-term, day-to-day blips.
Achievable: Evolutionary process from the base/present.	**Revolutionary:** Might require changes in personnel, organization, equipment, or philosophy.
Realistic: Within historical capability.	**Empowering:** Empowered to take calculated risks; capable of embracing failure, and of redefining the goals when you do fail.
Timely: Expected completion by a specific date, usually within 30 days.	**Tenacity:** Achieving the goal is more important than keeping to the anticipated delivery date. Very few transformational changes are done on time. Edison's inventing of the light bulb is an example of a transformative invention that took time.
	Controlled: Procedures and systems are in place for new performance levels. It's important to embed a new performance culture into the organization to avoid backsliding.
	Holistic: Likely to affect multiple organizations internally and externally.

Icon Co. made use of STRETCH goals in bringing forth the change they needed:

The traditional film manufacturing operations at *Icon Co.* had excess capacity. With six manufacturing lines available in any one week, typically only three lines needed to be run to meet the demand. The manufacturing lines were cumbersome to set up. They had hundreds of high-precision rollers the film would traverse and the film had to be coated and dried many times. Cleanliness was critical for photographic-based films. One dust spot, oil drip, or silicone spot could wreak havoc on the running and operational efficiency of the line causing knock-on effects for inventory, shipments, and cash management. It had been done this way for over fifty years.

The approach to scheduling lines was therefore to focus production on a line for one to two weeks and then switch production to a different line. Operational teams were, present 24/7 to operate production lines. Operating seven days a week twenty-four hours a day presents many challenges. Maintenance coverage, security, running heating, lights, coverage, and supervision: the list was extensive and costly.

A STRETCH goal was developed to try and operate the lines Monday to Friday twenty-four hours a day. The concept was to run more lines in a more concentrated approach. Production would start at 6 am on Monday with four lines and staff would run them nonstop all week until 10 pm on Friday. This had never been done before. Inevitably there was a healthy dose of skepticism, as experience suggested this would not work. Tradition dictated when a line was up and running, one should leave it alone. Now it was shut down on Friday and restarted on Monday morning.

The benefits of a changed production schedule, however, seemed to outweigh the historical reluctance. Closing operations each weekend resulted in considerable savings. Beyond the obvious cost savings, there were many other potential benefits: There was always a higher concentration of skilled staff available, and finding the technical, maintenance, and research support to cover weekends had proved challenging in the past. It was easier to meet quick order changes from customers because the additional production lines enabled responsiveness to the market. One element not expected was a sense of achievement every Friday at 10 pm when the production order book was closed, and the lines were shut off.

Soon *Icon Co.*'s operators became so good at running this way, they would beat the standard production targets and started finishing earlier on Fridays. *Icon Co.* ensured the shift that finished on a Friday was also the shift that had to start on a Monday morning. This assured continuity but also kept one team from leaving a mess for another team. Startups and shutdowns soon mirrored Formula One race car pit stops in efficiency.

There is an element of hope tied to STRETCH goals. Whereas the Vision is clear about what is projected, STRETCH goals are open-ended and carry an element of risk. *How will we reach the goals? Where will we fail? Will we discover new and better goals than the ones first contemplated? How will the STRETCH goals change the way we currently think and act?* STRETCH goals are inherently hopeful. Hope should not be confused with two different dynamics. The first is *wishing*. Wishing knows exactly what it wants. Hoping is risky and carries some uncertainty. When a leader says: "We will maintain an

8 percent gain year-over-year for the next three years," it is a wish. One wish is easily replaced by another wish, as letting go of a wish is rarely costly. The other dynamic is *daydreaming*—the mind wandering as often happens in childhood. Daydreaming rarely interacts with reality; it is just dreaming while not sleeping. Whereas the hope tied to stretch goals will lead to action, one can spend hours daydreaming without ever acting to bring about change. Daydreaming is often a defensive strategy undermining one's leadership as it distances one from one's employees, customers, and reality.

From a change management perspective you have the latitude to change around a Vision, SMART goal, STRETCH goal, Mission, or a Strategic Imperative. They are all part of taking a view of where you want to go and where you want to lead the organization.

Often change plans will fail; many reports and studies claim the failure rate for change plans is about 70%. Companies do fail. A recent study by a leading financial firm shows that after 5 years almost 50% of businesses fail (Table 5.3):[14]

Table 5.3 Business Failure Rates in the United States

Time frame	Percentage (%) of businesses that fail
Within 1 year	20.8
After 2 years	27.6
After 3 years	35.9
After 4 years	42.6
After 5 years	48.4
After 6 years	52.5
After 7 years	56.4
After 8 years	59.2
After 9 years	62.3
After 10 years	65.1

Predicting the future is impossible. How then can you analyze a goal, plan, vision, or strategy to see what the implications are of it becoming a reality in the future and how do you quantify the benefits and risks of the vision?

Discerning a Vision's Impact: A Case Study on Developing a Nuclear Battery

Imagine a stone thrown into a mirror-like lake or quiet pool. The mesmerizing ripple effect lasts much longer than one might expect, ever flowing wider. Inherent to discerning the Vision is to reckon *the ripple effect* of a decision, even one meant to bring change, can have. The core leadership team driving the change completes this exercise, often referred to as *rippling*. Here we imagine a company, *NuBatt*, is thinking about developing a nuclear battery. Though they are confident in their ability to develop one, they are uncertain of what its market impact will be. Rippling is throwing a nuclear-powered battery "stone" into the energy market "pool" and imagining what might happen.

Rippling, a term we prefer, has been described by others as Futures Wheels, Mind Mapping, Webbing, and Implication Wheels. The Futures Wheel concept was invented by Jerome C. Glenn in 1971, when he was still an education student, to imagine future consequences.[15] Rippling remains a simple but powerful technique to inform leadership discernment. It is an attempt to think forward or to consider the future implications of your action. How often do plans fail because we missed something obvious; we were blindsided or distracted by other things? How often do you find yourself saying, well with the benefit of hindsight that was obvious?

We can be so narrowly focused on a specific plan we can miss the obvious. A more open mindset can help us in our

leadership. A technique such as rippling provides a quantifi-
able method to consider what might happen when your goal
becomes a reality. It can help you "predict" or see potential
positives and negatives that you have not thought of. Once
you have greater insight on both positives and negatives, you
can enhance your plan to increase the chances of the positives and take "blocking" anticipatory action on the negatives.
It's akin to an ice hockey player anticipating where the puck is
going to be and/or where the defense is needed.

Join us in a thought experiment as we discern the consequences of a hypothetical goal: building a small nuclear
battery (see Figure 5.4). Play along. The only rule is that you
are not allowed to challenge the validity of the idea being
pursued. Bracket questions such as: What does it look like?
Or, is it technically possible? The rock we are throwing into
the proverbial pool is a nuclear battery. What will the ripple
effects be?

Regarding the battery:

Cost:	$3,000
Weight:	20 lbs.
Lifespan:	100 years
Power:	One battery can power a small engine, such as on a motorcycle or a lawnmower. Five batteries will power a car, boat, or small vehicle.
Maintenance:	$0.00 (o cost). However, it will cost $3,000 to recycle the radioactive ingredients at the end of the battery's life.

With the "rock" defined, the next step is to imagine throwing it into the system and discern the impact you think it will
have. As you start with the process of rippling, assemble a

team or group of people to consider this new product you have "launched." Remember this is an imaginative reality that cannot be challenged. Make sure your team has the specifications for the product, then invite them to ask clarifying questions so they can get their heads around exactly what this product is and is meant to accomplish. Give everyone some time on their own to think through what this now means. Your brainstorming will go better if everyone has had time to digest what the product is and consider what it might do to the system.

As you gather to brainstorm:

1. Place at the center the "rock" or event or product you want to think about. For our example, it is launching a consumer-oriented nuclear battery. Imagine the first ripple. Ask everyone to give you one or two impacts— those events occurring now that the battery is available to be purchased. Gather the impacts in a way for all to see.

2. Lead the team and rank the five most important impacts or likely events of those they generated that will happen when this battery enters the market. These are the first-order impacts—the first ripple effects—of the battery being launched into the market.
   Let's assume the five events the team wants to explore— all indicating the first ripple effect— as follows:
   I. The price of oil collapses.
   II. The price of uranium soars.
   III. Chaos ensues in the Middle East as oil prices collapse.
   IV. Green alternatives shut down as nuclear and cheap oil become available.
   V. A new industry is created to deal with disposing of nuclear waste.

3. Populate the first ripple with these events.

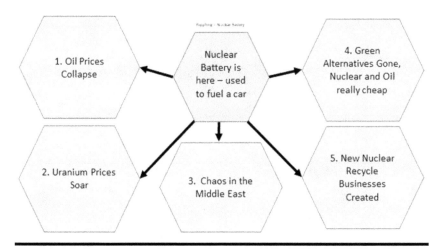

Figure 5.4 Ripple effect for a consumer nuclear battery.

Just as the ripple moves outward from the center, so does your ability to think forward increase. You now want to take each of the above events in turn and map it forward. The same rules apply: you are not allowed to question whether the event will happen or not. You have to accept it is now a reality. *What are the ripple effects of uranium prices soaring* (see Figure 5.5)? The brainstorming exercise by the team yields four events:

Let's think more about the ripple that uranium prices will increase with the launch of a nuclear battery:

1. Eastern Europe has become a global power as they have the second largest reserves of uranium (behind Australia).
2. Mining companies are the new oil companies making significant profits.
3. Other precious metal prices drop due to the extensive exploration for and mining of uranium.
4. Global wealth is redistributed according to the countries with the most uranium deposits. Australia, Kazakhstan, Canada, Namibia, and South Africa become the richest nations. America only comes in at #14.[16]

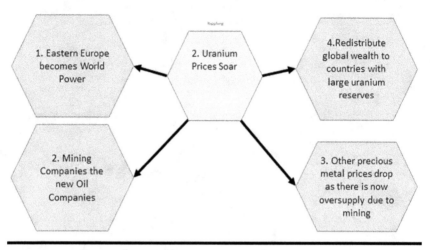

Figure 5.5   The expansive nature of rippling.

Now that you have mapped out the ripple effects of uranium prices soaring, you can repeat this exercise for every event. Working with a team is important: you need to generate and keep the energy around discerning the rippling effect, and such discernment takes significant effort and requires keeping a wide—gestalt-like—picture in mind to map each event forward. Thinking beyond your vision is hard work.

Let's work the ripple effect out one more ring and consider Eastern Europe becoming a world power due to its reserves in uranium. The group's discernment identified the following effects:

1. The Russian Federation reforms as Russia and its historic republics unite.
2. China and Africa join NATO to protect themselves against possible Russian Federation aggression.
3. Space exploration kicks off again, driven by the search for new sources of uranium.
4. The United States invents fusion energy reducing the dependency on uranium.

This is just one branch we have worked all the way to the third ripple. You and your team can now repeat the brainstorming for each of the ripples connected to uranium prices soaring and then once complete you move on and repeat for oil prices collapsing. In the true spirit of brainstorming there are no right or wrong answers and often one idea appearing sparks another divergent thought from another team member.

As you can see, thinking forward on this one aspect of uranium prices increasing results in many interesting possibilities to consider. It would be hard for any one person to grasp all of these at once and balance all the pros/cons in their head at the same time. The full impact of a low-cost 100-year consumer-oriented nuclear battery is significant. Each ripple leads to over 100 "effects" or impact events to consider. You could repeat this exercise with the different elements in the first ring, the first 1–5 positions on the mapping. There is technically no limit to the number of times you can repeat this exercise, each time thinking forward beyond your vision. However, like most things in life, there will be diminishing returns each time you repeat it.

You and your team can color code the mapping to identify particular effects that are of interest for further exploration, and those events you may want to stop or inhibit. Simple green for good, red for bad, and white for neutral can help visualize where the hot spots are. When you see green, you can invest in accelerating or increasing the probability of those effects coming true, and where you see red you can invest in trying to stop the event from coming true.

This rippling exercise—a way of thinking forward or beyond your Vision—can be repeated for many events that require leadership discernment. *Are you thinking of buying a hospital? Or create the next unicorn startup? Are you thinking of doing something new and extraordinary?* Start with the assumption you have bought the hospital and then, using the rippling exercise, think forward. Imagine your product is available and throw it into society. What might happen? You can look at good/bad events triggered and then decide how to enhance or mitigate each of them. Using this mapping tool you will be considering over 100 effects or events for any given "stone" thrown into a system. You will not work on all 100 elements, but the forward-thinking exercise will allow you to identify areas of weakness in your plan and areas of strengths. Having some forward visibility of these can increase your chances of success.

Working with a strong vision, STRETCH goals, and even rippling as a discernment process demand some level of self-differentiation. Revisit the scale (Chapter 3). Notice skills and traits such as: "Can discard old beliefs in favor of new ones," "[Are] not dogmatic or rigid in their thinking," and "Capable of listening to viewpoints of others with an open mind." Working with the Vision in creative and adaptive ways facilitates differentiated thinking, being broad-minded and less rigid.

"Vision," Friedman writes in his *Failure of Nerve*, "is generally thought of as a cerebral event. But the ability to see things differently and the effect of that ability on one's functioning—whether in art, science, or exploration—is an emotional phenomenon. It is having some sense of where you begin and end, and where others in your life end."[17] Vision is thus not only about communicating a destination or a picture for your institution: it is about you. As such, Vision is an important—but not the only—catalyst for change. The belief a Vision statement is the most important part of the change program, that clear communication of the Vision is all that's needed to guarantee change, is false. No amount of balloon blowing and cheerleading the new Vision will create change if people are comfortable with where they are or if they remain stuck in an emotional process resisting change. If a workforce is reactive, driven by the anxiety of what is happening or the pending changes, the more you, the leader, push the Vision, the stronger the resistance will be.

E: Ethics: Leading with Expressed Moral Convictions

Leadership is consequential. Your action will impact lives embedded in families and communities. The impact can be regional, national, or even global and ecological. When we ignore responsibility and ethics any change can be considered a success, even those bringing great harm to individuals, groups, or even the natural environment. Leading with no moral or ethical compass has had a devastating impact on individuals, organizations, societies, countries, and the environment. Examples of tyrannical changes abound. Ethics include not only social and relational standards and boundaries, but also financial, legal, moral, religious, and environmental considerations. What is often called the "golden rule of life"—do to others as you want to be done too, for what matters is how you live your life—is a strong foundation for ethical leadership. A few examples of ethical actions are as follows:

- In reducing the workforce, keeping individual needs in mind, and investing in redeployment.
- Honoring existing employment agreements as well as psychological "contracts."
- Seeking consistency across the organization for existing employees.
- Freezing executive compensation when employees receive little or no salary increases.

- Assuring recruits in a time of downsizing truly is critical to the future of the institution.
- Advancing employees who deserve a promotion.
- Increasing collaborative leadership around core decisions.
- Being fiscally responsible.
- Holding persons accountable for sexual and other boundary violations.

Often leaders work within contractual agreements when making changes. They "stick to" or "hide behind" the "law," interpreting those laws in a way that suits them. When leading change, it is important to look beyond the written agreements by which you might have to abide and to consider the psychological contracts existing in your community and even in the wider culture. Denise Rousseau, an organizational theorist who first elaborated on the values of a psychological contract, defines these contracts as follows: "The psychological contract encompasses the actions employees believe are expected of them and what response they expect in return from the employer."[18] This contract encompasses informal arrangements, mutual beliefs, and expectations, even perceptions between two parties.

A psychological contract is never static but evolves as communication changes between an employer and the employees. Effective and honest communication strengthens the psychological contract. When a contract is broken, such as when promises made regarding compensation or promotion are betrayed, or when decisions are made in ways denying transparency, the relational and emotional ethos of an institution is undermined. Before the leadership can blink, employees will disengage, possibly even sabotage the bottom line as turnover increases. With a broken employee contract, an institution will be unable to meet the expectations of its core stakeholders.

Leaders who create realistic, clear expectations for their employees are less likely to disappoint or be disappointed. These expectations need to admit that challenging situations or even adverse personal circumstances that will impact productivity can and do occur, without those situations leading to employees being blamed as incompetent or deviant. Sound psychological contracts always communicate and protect a sense of fairness. As *Icon Co.* sought a pivot, they discovered the importance of psychological contracts:

Icon Co. was faced with making a 50 percent reduction in employees as quickly as possible to reduce the financial losses being incurred. Rather than merely sticking to the law, the leadership put in place full-time redeployment resources and worked out a redeployment plan for every individual. This tailored approach generated significant trust and respect at all levels. In the short-term, leaders invested equal time and energy in helping the individuals being redeployed as they did in the remaining staff. It would have been easier to terminate 50 percent of the employees and move them off the payroll. The redeployment activities probably took twice as long to complete as going by the letter of the law would have done. Leaders made significant efforts to find individuals alternative work at *Chemical Co.*, the parent company. The staff who were selected to stay noticed. They saw their long-time colleagues and friends treated with respect and dignity and recognized the extra lengths to which the leadership team was going.

It was the tradition at *Icon Co.* for the managers to put on a Holiday celebration each year at the company social club—a combination of Monty Python humor and an opportunity to roast the executives. Even through the significant downsizing periods, the tradition continued. Ex-employees returned each year like distant family members to enjoy the show and most of all to relish the executives being roasted. It would be fair to say there were still some hard feelings over the reduction in the workforce. Many employees still believed they had suffered due to the errors of prior leaders and poor decision-making. However, there was a healthy level of respect for how the change had been managed. Although no one liked what had happened, by far the majority of those affected accepted everyone had been treated fairly, and even more than fairly.

R: Removing Resistance: Overcoming Every Action's Reaction

"At every crossroad on the path that leads to the future each progressive spirit is opposed by a thousand [people] appointed to guard the past," the playwright muses.[19]

Systems resist change because their emotional process seeks equilibrium and because every action has an equal and opposite reaction. In contemporary America addressing resistance has become a challenging, even precarious task most managers and leaders (would prefer to) avoid. *How does one call out those who are sabotaging the implementation of the Vision for change? How does one do so across lines of gender, race, and religion? How does one best respond to the social media pushback that will throw mud at you and your institution?* Managers are often poorly supported or even discouraged from dealing with difficult or hostile persons does not promote effective leadership. Leaders will often focus on the Vision and the Strategy and upsell these elements of the change program in the hope this will be sufficiently convincing to thwart resistance. Predictably, the exact opposite happens. The more you push your agenda, the more resistance grows. This creates an escalation on both sides and seldom results in a constructive way forward. What to do? Rather than being reactive to the resistance, prepare yourself to be responsive to what can be an opportunity for effective leadership.

Let's revisit how *Icon Co.*'s management reckoned with resistance:

When Icon Co. was negotiating with the unions to implement selective employment, there was the expected resistance. The unions claimed the testing process to select employees would be unfair, discriminatory, difficult, and not reflective of the skills needed to operate film manufacturing plants. Rather than simply pushing the agenda that this was the right thing to do, the leadership took the union representatives through a mock selection process. They gave them examples of the types of selective testing to be done. They even agreed to include service as one of the criteria for selection. They found most of the resistance and objections to the selection process were based on the fear of the unknown. Focusing on removing the resistance—the objections—of the union representatives enabled a more productive path forward.

The responses can be diagrammed as depicted in Table 5.4.

R: Removing Resistance

Table 5.4   Newton's Third Law—For Every Action, There Is an Equal and Opposite Reaction

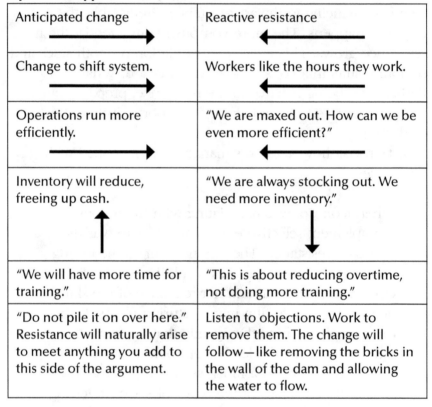

Anticipated change	Reactive resistance
Change to shift system.	Workers like the hours they work.
Operations run more efficiently.	"We are maxed out. How can we be even more efficient?"
Inventory will reduce, freeing up cash.	"We are always stocking out. We need more inventory."
"We will have more time for training."	"This is about reducing overtime, not doing more training."
"Do not pile it on over here." Resistance will naturally arise to meet anything you add to this side of the argument.	Listen to objections. Work to remove them. The change will follow—like removing the bricks in the wall of the dam and allowing the water to flow.

Addressing resistance in the right way has many profound benefits. If you start with the premise there is a good reason why people resist change, rather than just doing it to be disruptive or stubborn, you will be more successful. Disruptive resistance is typically the exception. Normally people are resisting for a good reason, even if that good reason is based solely on their vantage point. Therefore piling on the vision statements and the need for change from the leadership's view without considering why people are resisting leads to escalation and an impasse. The figure above illustrates how a simple change initiative such as changing working hours can have a major reaction. You can see how leadership could focus only on the left-hand side of the argument and the employees would continue to find counter-arguments.

Consider the forces at play here. Management is pushing from left to right. Employees are pushing back from right to left. If you can address and remove the forces pushing from right to left there is less and less resistance to the change you need. It is a bit like a dam and a river. The river is flowing from left to right and represents the change you want. The dam is the resistance stopping the river from flowing. If you can remove the dam, or at least open sluice gates, the river will flow more naturally. Work on removing clear obstacles.

An overlooked reason why persons resist change, directly implicating the emotional process, is experiencing loss. Since few families empower their members to engage loss constructively, leaving them with messages such as "Don't cry," "Tomorrow will be a better day," or even "Replace the loss as fast as possible," or "Time heals," your employees will likewise protect themselves from experiencing perceived or actual loss. All loss is painful. Ronald Heifetz and Marty Linksy, consultants and professors at the John F. Kennedy School of Government at Harvard University, argue that facilitating the work of mourning is a key leadership trait leaders should cultivate. In their *Leadership on the Line: Staying Alive Through the Dangers of Leading*, they simply state: "People do not resist change per se. People resist loss."[20] Be compassionate in your leadership and the resistance will diminish (see Chapter 4 on not being controlled by the emotional reactions of others).

All change is experienced as loss

Excursus: Leadership and the Work or Mourning

Heifetz and Linksy are correct: Systems and people do not resist change, they resist loss. Leaders who do not recognize this basic truth will be sabotaged in their efforts to bring change. Awareness of loss and how persons defend against loss should not be confused with the danger of empathy (see Chapter 4). Loss and grief call forth the compassion we recognize in excellent leaders. Many leaders distance themselves from the experience of loss, whether it is their losses or the losses they cause others to experience. One reason for this is that most families rarely recognize the losses their members experience, unless it is something tragic, such as the death of a patriarch or matriarch, or possibly the death of a child or younger family member. Lost hopes and dreams, for example, are rarely recognized as griefs. Ambiguous losses, such as infertility, early pregnancy loss, or the termination of a pregnancy, are rarely grieved openly. Some men never cry, seeing it as a sign of weakness. Leaders' loyalty to their families of origin creates blind spots around loss.

With all leaders tasked to bring change, loss becomes a stumbling block they have to overcome. Add to the personal and familial histories we bring a system's homeostatic resistance to change, and a leader can become stuck even before change sets in. The experience of loss does not judge whether a change is positive or negative and further complicates the matter. If a leader thinks their employees must follow them simply because they are introducing positive change, they will be blindsided by the resistance. Likewise, when a leader claims their authority over others to force change, the emotional process will undo those changes in good time.

Michael and Jennifer Armond built their family business, St. Luke Auditors, over the past 20 years as healthcare in the United States adopted managed care. They serve large, self-insured institutions that contract with insurance companies to manage the companies' health care accounts. As health care auditors, they have seen their business grow a great deal over the last years and now employ 35 auditors. Michael and Jennifer are thinking of retirement. They recognize their company functions like the mom-and-pop operation it once was and future growth would demand a culture change they do not want to oversee. The Armonds are in conversation with a competitor interested in a buyout. They secured higher salaries for their employees, guaranteed no one will lose their job for the first two years, competitive benefits, and assurances no one will be relocated. The Armonds have kept the best interests of their employees in mind and were thus surprised when few in the company were excited to learn about the buyout. Morale is low in the company, negative scenarios are offered, and crises are invented. The Armonds suddenly doubt whether they are doing the right thing and the purchaser is raising questions about the company's employees.

What seems to be a great deal on paper has become a tense situation that might thwart the buyout. The Armonds forgot losses cannot be replaced, only mourned and grieved. They ask their employees to accept significant losses determining the emotional process of the system:[21]

- **Relationship loss**: This is the loss experienced when opportunities end for relating to, sharing experiences and settling issues, and even fighting with, and otherwise being in the emotional and/or physical presence of a particular person. Adding persons to existing relationships, which will happen as two companies become one, can end current ways of relating and cause loss too.
- **Material loss**: The loss of a physical object or of familiar surroundings to which one has an important attachment. Material loss can be as simple as having to embrace the new company logo or getting a new email address. It includes working in new buildings and experiencing financial loss.

- **Intrapsychic loss**: The loss when expectations fail or possibilities never realize. It is the dying of dreams and dashed aspirations. For a mom-and-pop business to become a corporate entity is a significant intrapsychic loss. Employees who saw themselves as a family working for the Armonds for years, a buyout is both relational loss and intrapsychic loss.
- **Functional loss**: This grief is often associated with a person's body no longer functioning in healthy ways. Aging brings functional losses. Here, the Armonds indicate functional loss when they acknowledge they do not have the energy to continue to build their company. For their employees, how they are doing audits is likely to change.
- **Systemic loss**: The loss one experiences when one realizes one is no longer part of a system. Retirement always brings systemic loss, so too when a small, tight group is engulfed by a larger corporation.
- **Role loss**: The loss awakened when a specific social role ends. The Armonds as entrepreneurs who built a company face this loss. The employees of St. Luke Auditors have specific roles and "places" in the company, personalities accepted and mostly tolerated by all. They now wonder whether the new company would need two people doing the same job.

Since loss changes one's identity, one can assume that the Armonds and their employees are confused about who they are.

Should you be a consultant to the Armonds, how would you proceed to assure the best possibility the buyout moves forward? How does one engage in the corporate work of mourning? How will you facilitate the formation of a new identity for individuals and teams as one company is integrated into another? The work of mourning is "to reckon, to recount, relate, or narrate, to consider, judge, or evaluate, even to estimate, enumerate, and calculate [the loss occurred]."[22] This work takes time. It demands significant leadership listening to how change is experienced when dominant leadership, seeking to close the buyout, comes more naturally to leaders.

If the Armonds could facilitate town hall meetings where their employees can vent their fear and frustration, and their sense of loss, one can expect a shift in the emotional process. Rational assurances that the takeover is to everyone's benefit will not succeed. If the Armonds cannot receive the hostility coming their way without being defensive, they need a consultant or mentor to facilitate or empower them to differentiate and remain significant and less anxious to their staff. They can explore *the way it is* versus *the way it should* or could be as we explored above. Thus, *the way it should be*: "We should accept this buyout because it is the rational best decision for all." *The way it is*, however, is "We are anxious about the planned buyout as we will lose the close-knit family operation we have become." Significant leaders will go deep with the way it is.

A certain paradox of a system's emotional process is when *the way it is* is explored by a significant leader, the gap or distance between the two opposing scenarios diminishes. There will be less anxiety in the system. Remember, employees do not resist change, they resist loss. When a significant leader explores the losses asked of employees, the exploration does not imply moving forward with a difficult decision should be abandoned. Rather, the compassion the leader adds to the system by engaging the diverse nature of loss will increase the likelihood that persons who resisted a change can be partners in the change. Rituals, such as creating a wall of remembrance or even a company book, and celebrating the growth of their company, can further assist in giving loss a voice. Once the emotional process, now colored by loss becomes less anxious, persons may be able to find peace in a future under new leadership.

Communicate the Desired Vision

Beyond understanding change implies a loss, remember to state the change you want and why it is important, and then engage with staff to record any objections (resistance) they have to this change. This can be done as exercises in groups and teams. Get the teams to articulate why the change cannot take place. Record all objections without judgment. Once you have recorded the objections, start working with the team on ideas and activities removing their resistance or objections. You will find that when one person objects there will be another person in the room who thinks they can solve it. People like showing off their capacity to solve someone else's problems.

With the Armonds the sense of loss was clear. Sometimes the resistance is more superficial and you need to dig deeper to understand the concern. The noise is trying to point you somewhere else. Recall that the initial resistance of the unions at *Icon Co.* to selective employment was based on the fear of the unknown, although no one was willing to say they feared the process. Once they experienced a mock exercise, their resistance waned significantly.

If you explore why people are resisting change and try to eliminate the resistance, many other things are likely to happen. You start to demonstrate you are less anxious and can listen nondefensively to others rather than just driving your agenda. If you respond to their concerns and can find solutions, you'll build trust and respect. Most of the time we all understand why change needs to take place. But we are typically wrapped up in our own needs and fears. In general, employees are resisting institutional change because of personal reasons, not primarily because they disagree with the vision you present. Finally, remember those who are resisting change might be right. Their resistance might be well founded. Perhaps they are trying to tell you that you're about to make a mistake.

Leaders who listen to and remove sources of resistance encounter a variety of situations:

- Staff is resisting new scheduling since they have childcare responsibilities. Finding alternative placement opportunities within the institution or department can remove this resistance.
- Employees are resisting change because they realize they cannot meet new expectations. Empower and equip the employees with new skills.
- Employees are experiencing loss of a title, for example, as job descriptions shift. Allow collaboration in structuring the new organizational chart.
- Staff is resisting change because they are expecting to lose their jobs. While still under contract, move staff to a redeployment pool until they find new employment.
- Employees are resisting because their roles and functions will disappear in the new vision. Protect technical and other expertise in the company.
- Persons have a strong emotional bond with a particular building, a way of doing things, or even an object such as a manual, book, or piece of equipment. Host town hall meetings where employees can vent their emotions, remember and tell about their experiences, and perhaps create a ritual to honor the loss and pending change.
- A team resists because they will not be needed in the new structure. Recognize specific teams with a plaque or even a named room. Redeploy those affected.
- Employees may resist and actively sabotage the process. Terminating the contracts of these employees might be the only path forward. Without termination, such employees may recruit others to join them and frustrate your attempts at moving the organization forward. Regardless of how much one works to overcome resistance, some sabotage will remain in the system.

One of the most significant forms of unspoken resistance is passive-aggressive behavior. This describes employees or team members circling quietly like sharks below the surface just waiting for the sniff of "failure" in the water. Describing someone as passive-aggressive is a bit like calling someone "happy sad." The term is an oxymoron. You are dealing with passive, distant anger. You could consider passive anger and aggressive anger as two extreme swings of a wrecking ball. Imagine you have a wrecking ball and you pull it up to the left (see Table 5.5 and Figure 5.6 below). Held in this position, you have all this anger stored up. Release the wrecking ball and watch it destroy everything in its path. Pull the ball to the right and you have aggressive anger or energy stored up. Release the wrecking ball from here and it does as much damage as passive anger. Both passive and aggressive anger wreck relationships, teams, organizations, and companies equally.

Aggressive anger is typically not tolerated. People recognize it, call it out, and have very low or zero tolerance for it. It is much harder to eliminate passive anger, which is just as damaging but much harder to identify and deal with. One way to protect yourself against aggressive anger is to differentiate between you being a flesh-and-blood leader (you as a person) and being a leader who mostly resides in the minds of others (the "you" or leader they imagine you to be). Of course, you are not an imagined person only, but someone who feels deeply and who leads with confidence. Every person has an internalized image of who a leader should be formed over many years and numerous experiences of leadership. Reminding yourself the anger from someone else is most often directed at their internalized image of you as a leader can lessen the hurt and reactivity you may experience when dealing with aggressive anger.

It is better to operate from a position of self-differentiated assertiveness. This is not easy to achieve and/or sustain in organizations with passive and aggressive behavior characteristics, but possible. Passive people often view assertive leaders as aggressive, as they don't shirk conflict. Aggressive people, in turn, often find assertive leaders passive as they don't respond in anger. Assertive leaders don't just roll over and play dead like passive people. They have an uncanny knack for standing up to aggressive people without getting angry. Such a move often increases the anger in an aggressive person.

How can we distinguish assertive leadership from aggressive or passive leadership?

Table 5.5   Assertive Leadership

Assertive leader	Aggressive leader	Passive leader
Validates others' feelings and views, but clearly states the commitment to move forward.	Communicates: "Do as you are told."	Ignores disgruntled employees.
Offers calm reinforcement.	Tends to be angry and loud.	Is silent.
Steps out of triangles.	Controls triangles.	Tends to be stuck in triangles.
Seeks closeness.	Forces closeness; often violates physical boundaries.	Is enmeshed in systems.
Is vulnerable.	Ridicules those presenting feelings.	Is a victim or stays in denial.
Is authentic.	Protects a/their persona.	Is compliant.
Is less anxious under pressure.	Adds destructive anxiety to the system: "You're fired"; engages in physical altercations and yelling and screaming.	Is paralyzed under pressure.

To be assertive is to be differentiated, confident, bold, assured, and even forthright. Such a leader exudes inner authority and competence without being pushy or domineering. Assertive leaders don't mind telling someone they disagree with them. In some companies and cultures, this is taboo and is seen as an act of aggression. If a "kumbaya" mentality—let's all get along—is the order of the day, then being confident and forthright indeed comes across as being aggressive. Passive people need to be invited to the surface, rather than bare their teeth below the surface. Knowing who the aggressive types are is easy; they don't lurk under the surface.

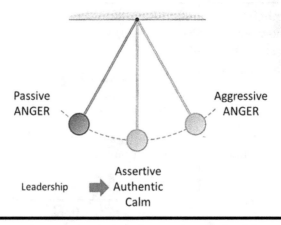

Figure 5.6   Passive, aggressive, and assertive leadership.

Let's expand on the thoughts contained by Figure 5.6:

Aggressive anger: Anger expressed in this way is directed at the other person and intends to hurt others emotionally, physically, or psychologically. It seeks to marginalize others relationally to disempower them. Yelling, put-downs, and hitting are extreme examples of aggressive anger.

Passive anger: A person internalizes the expression of anger when they avoid dealing with the situation contributing to feelings of anger. The anger can then be expressed by getting even, holding a grudge, slowing down processes ("quiet quitting"), or being mean at some point in the future. Spreading nasty rumors and gossiping, not speaking up, and damaging property can be examples of passive anger too.

Assertive calmness: It is the differentiated leader. Think of assertiveness as being a place of calm and strength. The wrecking ball has come to rest in a neutral position. In the passive and aggressive position, it is raised with stored energy ready to wreak havoc. Assertiveness uses "I-language" and focuses on what can be observed, rather than focusing on a person's character traits, for example. "I feel frustrated when I see the topics on the agenda are changed without prior notice" or, "I am disappointed when I feel disconnected in a relationship". Using "I-language" is usually the best way to communicate and avoids resistive "you" triggers. Try having an argument with someone without using the word "you".

Removing resistance is a skill all leaders must master. Remaining present in challenging conversations, walking toward conflict when others seek to avoid it, but also growing a compassionate heart reckoning that your leadership will induce loss are all arts a leader can and must practice. Leading in this way is "easier" if your level of self-differentiation is growing and you have someone that encourages, supports, and empowers and protects you—someone we call a sponsor.

S: Having a Sponsor: The Gift of Support, Experience, and Wisdom

We've reached the final element of DRIVERS: having a sponsor. We guess looking back on your leadership, those times when you felt on top of your game included a senior leader or another person who functioned as a mentor, an advisor, or a wise sage and guide. A sponsor is someone who empowers you to implement change and who supports and creates an environment welcoming change. Though a person outside your organization can play this role too, their ability to create an atmosphere of change in your institution is limited. We thus imagine a senior executive or administrator in your organization holding the position of being your sponsor or support.

Specialists in change management, consulting firm Prosci identifies "active and visible executive sponsorship" as a best practice of executives and senior leaders alongside practices such as structuring change, communicating frequently, engaging frontline employees, and supporting middle managers.[23] In Prosci's research, sponsorship emerged as the highest-ranked contributor to success in change management, with a lack of executive support being the biggest obstacle. The primary sponsor is the executive who can authorize the change, the person who holds ultimate responsibility for the institution's growth and success. The higher the risk for an institution, the more senior the sponsor needs to be. Low-risk change can benefit from a mid-level manager as the sponsor. And sometimes more than one sponsor is needed, especially if complex changes are sought.

A sponsor:

- Supports the change you seek to facilitate by giving consistent attention to the change and the need for change management.
- Leads, motivates, and equips—champions—others in the organization to embrace the change.
- Aligns priorities of resources and people in the organization to make instrumental decisions regarding the change.
- Communicates with the project management and change management teams, remains accessible during the process of change, and addresses resistance to the change.
- Calls, influences, and builds coalition with others on the executive leadership team to maintain buy-in and participate in a coalition of sponsorship.

Unsurprisingly, Prosci's research shows the higher the percentage of effective sponsorship, the higher the possibility of successful change. More than 50% of leaders responsible for change indicate their executives have some understanding of their role as a sponsor.

Ready to Lead?

As a leader, you want to bring change. DRIVERS highlights core leadership principles and practices when change is sought: dissatisfaction, recruiting critical mass; initial step(s); vision; ethics; resistance; and (having a) sponsor. DRIVERS complement a systems approach to leadership. You have likely witnessed or experienced many a failed attempt at facilitating change. Engaging the DRIVERS discussed in this chapter will assist you in being the kind of leader you want to be, one who can lead a system toward sustained transformation, and doing so being less anxious.

Change, the aphorism states, is 1% inspiration and 99% perspiration.[24] We agree.

Notes

1. Ibid., 246–247.
2. As quoted in the Harvard Business Review. See: https://hbr.org /2000/05/cracking-the-code-of-change. Accessed August 13, 2021.
3. Andrew Sturdy and Christopher Grey, "Beneath and Beyond Organizational Change Management: Exploring Alternatives," *Organization* 10, no. 4 (2003): 651.
4. An Accenture study quoted in Siobhan Sutherland Rogers, "Change Management: Your Roadmap to Training Success," *Training and Development in Australia* 40, no. 3 (2013): 4–6.

5. John P. Kotter, *Leading Change* (Cambridge: Harvard Business Review Press, 2012), 40.
6. See: https://en.wikipedia.org/wiki/Kodak. Accessed August 13, 2021.
7. The language of significant and dominant leadership, and "the way it is" and "the way it should be" is adapted from research on the care of persons who are depressed. See: Silvano Arieti and Jules Bemporad, *Psychotherapy of Severe and Mild Depression* (Northvale: J. Aronson, 1993), 109–28.
8. Gen. Powell's presentation can be found in the Homeland Security Digital Library: https://www.hsdl.org/?abstract&did=467329. Accessed August 16, 2021.
9. Everett M. Rogers, *Diffusion of Innovations*, 5th ed. (New York: Free Press, 2003), 245.
10. Adapted from: ibid., 260, 320.
11. Bowen, *Family Therapy in Clinical Practice*, 325.
12. James O. Prochaska and Janice M. Prochaska, *Changing to Thrive: Using the Stages of Change to Overcome the Top Threats to Your Health and Happiness* (Center City: Hazelden Publishing, 2016). Prochaska identifies the phases of "Precontemplation" (initial thoughts about first steps and the need for change and a wish for change), "Contemplation" (not quite ready to take a first step; this phase includes research and analysis), "Preparation" (getting ready for the first step), "Action" (taking that first step), and "Maintenance" (which can take up to six months or longer before actions show any effectiveness). Prochaska advises us to envisage a "Termination" date for our first steps, that moment at which the step taken has become the new normal.
13. The line can be found on George Harrison's song, "Any Road" from the posthumously released album, *Brainwashed* (2002). The song was Harrison's final single. See: https://www.george-harrison.com/releases/brainwashed/. See also: https://www.rollingstone.com/music/music-album-reviews/brainwashed-186904/. Accessed July 4, 2023.
14. From LendingTree Analysis of U.S. Bureau of Labor Statistics (BLS) Data. See: https://www.lendingtree.com/business/small/failure-rate/. Accessed July 2, 2023.

15. For the history of the Futures Wheel, see: Jerome C. Glenn, "Futurizing teaching vs. futures courses" in *Social Science Record* 9 (3), 26–29. And, Jerome C. Glenn, "The Futures Wheel," *Futures Research Methodology* 3 (2009): 1. For Joel Barker's Implication Wheel, see: https://www.implications-wheel.com/ (Accessed October 2023). For Mind Mapping and Webbing, see: Tony Buzan, *Use Your Head* (London: BBC Publications. 1974); Tony Buzan and Chris Griffiths. *Mind Maps for Business: Using the Ultimate Thinking Tool to Revolutionise How You Work*. 2nd Edition (New York: Pearson, 2014).

16. See: https://www.worldatlas.com/articles/the-largest-uranium-reserves-in-the-world.html.

17. Friedman, *A Failure of Nerve: Leadership in the Age of the Quick Fix*, 235.

18. Denise M. Rousseau and Martin M. Greller, "Human Resource Practices: Administrative Contract Makers," *Human Resource Management* 33, no. 3 (1994): 386.

19. Belgian playwright and Nobel laureate, Maurice Maeterlinck Quoted in: Gabriella C. Weaver et al., eds., *Transforming Institutions: 21st Century Undergraduate Stem Education* (West Lafayette: Purdue University Press, 2016), 197.

20. Ronald A. Heifetz and Marty Linsky, *Leadership on the Line: Staying Alive Through the Dangers of Leading* (Boston: Harvard Business School Press, 2002), 11.

21. Adapted from: Kenneth R. Mitchell and Herbert Anderson, *All Our Losses, All Our Griefs: Resources for Pastoral Care*, 1st ed. (Philadelphia: Westminster Press, 1983).

22. Jacques Derrida, Pascale-Anne Brault, and Michael Naas, *The Work of Mourning* (Chicago: University of Chicago Press, 2001), 2.

23. See: https://www.prosci.com/resources/articles/primary-sponsors-role-and-importance and https://www.prosci.com/resources/articles/change-management-best-practice. Accessed August 16, 2021.

24. Modern aphorism based on Thomas Edison's famous statement: "Genius is one percent inspiration and 99 percent perspiration."

Chapter 6

Reckoning the Cost of Decisions Taken: Mitigating the Risks in Change

As a leader, how confident are you that your decisions will result in success? Leaders rarely admit this, but many of their decisions, also the ones they do not make, are a roll of the dice; they may or may not lead to expected outcomes. Poorly differentiated leaders are more likely to take their chances, hoping against hope that success will follow them. Why would success reward poor leadership?

Excellent leadership and transformation are synonymous. This transformation begins with the leader's self-differentiation. An organization will never grow beyond the level of self-differentiation of its leaders. The invisible loyalty within the homeostatic principle guarantees a system's or organization's emotional process is maintained. Overcoming this resistance is always needed for change to occur. Self-differentiated leaders avoid the either/or paradox; they engage with the organization

 DOI: 10.4324/9781003463993-10

without becoming triangulated into the emotional processes and they can be empathic yet independent. A key attribute of a self-differentiated leader is the capacity to admit when they are wrong. Highly self-differentiated leaders are more interested in the cost of being wrong than of being right. They recognize they make mistakes and are curious about how big a mistake they might make, if they are wrong.

You have seen a leader or leadership team stuck between divergent choices, both seemingly good. How does one lead through polarized differences? Congruent with Bowen and Friedman who saw Western society as increasingly anxious, polarization is merely a symptom of togetherness forces and a drive for individuality that lost touch with one another. "The climate of contemporary America," Friedman writes, "has become so chronically anxious that our society has gone into an emotional regression that is toxic to well-defined leadership."[1] Across all societal spheres we are most often led by anxious, poorly differentiated leaders.

Self-differentiated leaders lead differently, remain less anxious, and facilitate change. *But how does one bring change in a situation where opposite ideas are being offered? How does one reach consensus enough for a team or organization to move forward?* That an anxious system presents polarized views to its leaders should not surprise anymore. It is, after all, the unconscious response of the emotional process. We are reminded of *Hewlett-Packard Enterprise* executive, Meg Whitman, who said: "The price of inaction is far greater than the cost of making a mistake."[2]

Leaders do and perform; they act and make decisions. It may be the only trait every leader—good or bad—shares. Not all leaders, however, feel empowered to make decisions. We often hear: "That decision is above my pay grade;" "They do not pay me enough to tackle this." Statements such as these understand every decision taken contains elements of resistance, risk, and reward. Leaders intuitively know all decisions are praised and (rightly) criticized. They protect themselves from the latter—remember leaders feel all emotions deeply— for criticism stings. A leader so well-protected that they do not feel professional pushbacks and criticisms will have a compromised personal and relational life.

Mature emotional processes take informed action

We all make mistakes, we are human, after all. Many leaders would gladly recall the decisions they made: the leadership of *Western Union* passing on the telephone, those who led *America Online's* merger with *Time Warner,* the leaders behind *Kodak* not acting on the digital revolution, those at *Decca Records* not signing *The Beatles, Excite's* leadership passing on acquiring *Google* when it was only a search engine, and *Blockbuster Video* passing on *Netflix.* Meg Whitman became CEO of *Quibi* after she left *HP. Quibi* was meant to be a new streaming service. It was founded in August 2018 and closed in October 2020 having burnt through $1.75b of venture capital. Some mistakes come with a huge price tag. Whereas some leadership teams made regrettable decisions, others celebrate the choices they made: *Apple, Inc.* re-hiring Steve Jobs, *Exxon* merging with *Mobil,* and *Disney* merging with *Pixar/Marvel.*

Decisions are of course easy to characterize in hindsight. The alternative for *Decca Records* was to sign every artist or band walking into the room. How could one tell which one would be a success? Signing every band was and still is not practical. *Excite* passing on *Google* ... Had *Excite* bought *Google,* would *Google* have gone on to achieve web-based search dominance, or would they have gotten lost in a larger corporation? One could argue the same for *Blockbuster* and *Netflix.* If *Blockbuster* had bought *Netflix,* would they have stayed with postal returns of DVDs? One could argue Netflix went on to bigger and better things because it remained independent. Likewise, Steve Jobs' return could have ended much like his first tour of duty at *Apple, Inc.* Who could call the outcome in advance?

Leaders often get caught up in thinking they are right, believing they know what is best, and that they (alone) have a handle on the truth. Departments, companies, nonprofits, leadership teams, boards, and even faith communities can easily experience groupthink and get caught up in the belief they are right about their discernments. We do this as individuals too, demonstrating remarkable stubbornness in our opinions or views about what is right or wrong, forgetting our unique vantage points inform our views. In writing this book, we had many conversations and work sessions. Often we admitted we are seeing the world differently as individuals, also compared to most other leaders. In a state of confirmation bias toward our ideas, we sent off a draft of the book to an editor. Her red pen led to a complete redraft of the book, leaving chapters on the cutting floor. The togetherness forces in a system promotes relationships between people who agree, who think alike, act alike, even look like, and often are of the same socio-economic class.

Leaders reckon the cost of their decisions

Leadership Discernment = Recognizing the Cost of Being Wrong

When confronted with a big decision about the future, it is sometimes more insightful to consider the cost of being wrong rather than the benefit of being right. Leadership is more about financial cost and reward than about risk and reward. Risk and reward expose our tendency to think in binary forms: good or bad, yes or no, left or right, take it or leave it, presence or absence, togetherness or individuality. Of course, many other cultural binaries can be named. French philosopher Jacques Derrida reminds us such thinking leads to "binary oppositions" where "one of the two terms governs the other ... or has the upper hand."[3] With a winner and a loser, Derrida advises we deconstruct all binaries and find a way to "neutralize" the binary "in practice" and overturn it, mindful that "the hierarchy of dual oppositions always reestablishes itself."[4] Reckoning the cost of a decision rather than thinking in terms of it being the right or wrong decision can break the binary. Most leaders do not reckon the financial cost of their decisions, falling back on trying harder, looking for answers when they need to reframe the question, or relying blindly on luck a decision will pay off. Leadership built on poor discernment cannot be sustained beyond possible short-term success. *How much luck do you need to succeed?* Fortune favors the prepared; catastrophe awaits those who confuse luck with strength. Is it better to be prepared for what does not happen than to be unprepared for what does?

There are four possible outcomes for any one decision you make: The first outcome is you were right. Note the use of "were right." You will only know you are right with the benefit of hindsight. You might think, with no doubt, you *are* right, or better said, *going to be* right. But you will not know for sure until after the event when you can look back with glowing pride. When we are making decisions, we don't know the outcome of our decisions; you don't get to pick truth.

A second outcome is you were wrong about the decision you made. You made a mistake and the actions you took might be leading to a bigger mess than had you left things alone. Maybe you hired a person who is a poor fit for the position they hold; perhaps a merger is failing; national and international trends undid your contextual discernment; your plan for turning the numbers around is not working. In hindsight you regret making a particular decision and your inner critic is loud to remind you of what you should have done.

The third outcome is to decide on a plan of action only to begin to doubt it and ultimately abandon it, either for a new plan or nothing at all, no action. Now it appears your original thoughts and plan were correct. You should have stayed with the first plan. You passed on *The Beatles* after initially thinking they were great, and now, with the benefit of hindsight, you should not have passed on them. This is often referred to as the missed opportunity, the stock that is now on a bull run, you should have bought. You are kicking yourself and again your inner critic has a field day.

The fourth possible outcome is you were right not to pursue the idea or plan. You are relieved you had second thoughts and decided not to proceed. *The Spiders* were nothing like *The Beatles* and you were right not to sign them, as tempting as the opportunity was. You sigh in the reassurance you can still make a good decision. You still have it. Good call to reject the idea.

The outcomes of the decisions we make are impossible to call in advance

Rather than assuming or hoping you are right, it is more effective to assess the financial cost and risk of being wrong: *What is the cost of being wrong by either proceeding with the decision or passing on it? How much risk am I asking my institution or team to take?* Weighing up the cost of being wrong in the decision you took or passing on the right one to implement a poor choice, for example, can help you quantify how much *risk* you are taking. If the risks are high it might merit doing some more work before you lead your institution or the team down that path.

As you make a decision to either proceed or reject a plan or idea, either option can be right or wrong. Think of this as Right and Wrong with Plan 1 or Right and Wrong with Plan 2. A good example of processing decisions in this way are legal trials.

In a legal system such as in the United States where everyone is presumed innocent until found guilty, error cost analysis gives insight into how legal decisions are made. Imagine a person on trial for shoplifting, accused of stealing a $1,000 watch:

- *Right 1*: The defendant is found innocent; we release the individual. The jury was correct in the individual's innocence.
- *Wrong 1*: The defendant is found innocent and is released. But the jury got it wrong: the individual was guilty and the jury should not have found them innocent: the individual is released back into society and steals again.
- *Right 2*: The defendant was found guilty. It is true the defendant was guilty, and the jury was correct to reject their claims of innocence. The individual is jailed.
- *Wrong 2*: The defendant is found guilty and is convicted. But the jury got it wrong: the individual was innocent and unjustly convicted. The system has now incarcerated an innocent individual.

Acknowledging there are two possible wrong outcomes with every decision we make, not just one wrong, is a good place to start. We now attribute a cost to the wrong decisions and weigh how much risk we are taking about the decision we are about to make. We want to weigh up the error cost of *Wrong 1* to the error cost of *Wrong 2*. *Do the error costs indicate we need to be 90% confident of our decision or 10%? You* do not know whether the defendant is guilty or innocent. A jury and a judge provide an opinion, their opinions are just that, opinions. They can rule an innocent person guilty and vice versa. You can, however, weigh the evidence and make your best judgment.

Let's revisit the possibilities of each outcome:

Wrong 1: Finding the defendant innocent when they are guilty.

- Let's assume the defendant steals another watch with a value of $1,000 and then you have the cost to arrest and charge them again.
- If the trial costs $20,000, the total cost is thus $21,000 per case brought forward. Since justice was not served the first time, the total cost is the cost of the first watch and trial and the second that will follow, making the error cost of $42,000.

Wrong 2: Finding the defendant guilty when they were innocent.

- The shame and embarrassment are overwhelming for the individual. An innocent individual was convicted of shoplifting a $1,000 watch.
- Being wrongly convicted of a crime could have a significant domino effect on someone's life. Maybe the person starts to drink as they self-medicate. This leads to them losing their job. Their relational life implodes due to the addiction that has formed. They end up being alienated from their partner and children and cannot pay child support.
- The wrongly convicted individual eventually recovers, gets over their challenges, and gets back to a normal functioning life. This takes them five years at an estimated

cost of $2,000,000. This estimate comes from the loss of earnings, court cases to appeal the initial verdict, and the personal cost of divorce and family alienation.

We can now evaluate the confidence level by comparing the two costs in a ratio:
The confidence level is the cost of *Wrong 1* divided by the cost of *Wrong 1* and *Wrong 2*. The equation is thus:

$$\$42,000 \div (\$42,000 + \$2,000,000) = 2\%$$

In the case of the potential shoplifter, we can say one has to be only 2% confident the person is innocent. The cost of wrongly convicting someone for stealing a watch which they did not steal is significantly more than the cost of letting a guilty shoplifter go free. This is one reason why petty crimes rarely result in jail time or convictions, particularly for first offenders.

Truth is discerned from the evidence provided, evidence is easily tainted. A judge or jury, or in this case you, only have to be 2% confident in the decision. Alternatively, you could look at this example and say you needed to be 98% confident they are guilty before convicting them. There would need to be overwhelming evidence the individual you have before you is indeed the watch thief. Often this comes from convicting repeat offenders rather than first-time offenders. Repeated patterns of behavior would increase your confidence in a conviction.

When the Stakes Are Higher

Imagine a second courtroom, this one a murder trial. With murder, the impact on society increases exponentially compared to a watch shoplifter. Releasing a killer in error could result in another murder—possibly even several murders.

We are weighing up the error costs in the same way we did in the first courtroom. You will either find the person innocent and this can either be *Right or Wrong*. Equally you can find the person guilty and you could be *Right or Wrong*. The math, however, is much different and indicates why murder trials are conducted the way they are.

- *Right 1*: You conduct the trial and the defendant is found innocent. This is the right outcome.
- *Wrong 1*: The defendant is put on trial, found to be innocent, and set free. However, the individual is guilty, released into society, and promptly commits another murder. With a cost to life estimated to be $10m, plus court costs of $200,000, a murder trial's cost is $10.2m.[5] Since justice was not served the first time, the total error cost is therefore $20.4m.
- *Right 2:* The individual is found guilty and charged with murder. This is the correct decision and the individual goes to prison.
- *Wrong 2*: We reject their innocence and convict someone for a murder they did not commit. Let's assume there is no death penalty, and the individual is sent to prison and eligible for parole after 30 years. The person now has no job, gets divorced, and serves 30 years in prison. Let's assume the cost of being wrong in this scenario is $5m. About half the cost of human life.

What is the confidence level in this courtroom? The confidence level is *Wrong 1* divided by the cost of both *Wrong 1* and *Wrong 2*:

$$\$20.4m \div (\$4m + \$20.4m) = 80\%$$

Thus, you now must be 80% confident this individual is innocent. Compared to the first courtroom where you only had to be 2% confident the individual was innocent. The cost of being wrong has gone up significantly. You have to be 40 times more confident about your decision in a murder trial than in a shoplifting trial. For this reason, murder trials take much longer and require much more effort to reach a verdict.

Despite the starting principle being the same—innocent until proven guilty—you can see the burden on proof of innocence is different when you look at these two examples through the lens of error costs. If you have to be 80% confident in your decision of innocence in a murder trial you can see why people might more frequently be found guilty, in error, for murder trials than they would be for shoplifting.

The legal system tries to mitigate this error by calling forth more evidence, relying on expert witnesses, DNA testing, jury selection, and more. Because the outcome error is so significant, the legal system is working to lower the risk of getting it wrong. Although you might assume you are innocent until proven guilty, in the case of murder trials, the embedded behavior of the courtroom system feels more like you are *guilty until proven innocent.* The system is working hard to avoid a wrong decision and release a guilty person back into society. A person wrongly charged with murder will need a good lawyer. Trials have been taking place for thousands of years. The error costs principles are well ingrained into the behavior and practices in the courtroom as lawyers and judges apply the principles of error cost without even thinking about the process itself, in unconscious ways.

Institutions Need to Reckon with the Cost of Their Decisions

Contrast our hypothetical court cases with business or organizational decisions. *How often do you think departments, organizations, and companies apply the same kind of rigor to their decisions? If you were to work out the confidence level in one of your decisions and it came out at 80%, would you proceed in your discernment process with the same rigor and testing of the discernment process found in murder trials? How many mergers, acquisitions, and investments fail due to a "blind faith" belief in one's decision?* Many leaders are so convinced they are right about their big, bold decisions that they often skip the analysis or reflection on the decision they are about to make. Leaders are not trained to think *Right, Wrong, Right, Wrong.* Most leaders might only make two or three big decisions in their life. These decisions might need the same rigor applied to them as a murder trial. Faced with a big decision about the future, it would be wise for a leader to explore the cost of being *Wrong* rather than just being confident about being *Right.* Calculating the confidence level of the decision you are about to make based on the financial cost of errors is simple to do. A more robust, less risky process would be to gather a team to collectively analyze the error costs associated with either advancing with the decision and getting it wrong or rejecting it and losing out on the opportunity.

Wrong 1, the cost of proceeding and getting it wrong. This is the cost of doing the merger and it does not work. What is the downside, lost share value, employee turnover, lost customers, lost revenue? This could be significant. Some of the biggest mergers and acquisition failures include: *America Online* and *Time Warner* (2001)—$65 billion, *Daimler-Benz* and *Chrysler* (1998)—$36 billion, and *Kmart* and *Sears* (2005)—$11 billion.[6] The decision does not have to be a merger. It could be a decision to move into a new market, launching a new type of product, exiting a market or country, or using an A-list personality or rock star to promote your company, brand, or product. What can go wrong?

Wrong 2, calculating lost revenue you would have gained, lost shareholder value, lost profit, or lost market share you would have gained if you decide not to proceed with the plan. This is the opportunity cost or value of rejecting the plan. If the plan "Right 1" is to merge and you think the increase in value from the merger is $1b, then this is the opportunity lost if you reject it. This is *Wrong 2*. You reject the $1billion improvement plan.

When the error cost, *Wrong 1*, is much greater than the error in rejecting the opportunity, *Wrong 2*, it is always wise to pause and do some more homework. If you still want to proceed with the plan, you need to lower the risk of the decision you are about to make, and you should approach it with the same rigor as a murder trial.

Gather more evidence and slow down the process. Study institutions and companies that made similar decisions. Being more optimistic, more forceable, and more determined to be right, is not a good business strategy. If you are pursuing an acquisition and the error cost is high, you could purchase a small stake in the company rather than buying the whole company in one go. Working on lowering the risk of being wrong will generate better outcomes than trying to convince everyone you are right.

Getting your team involved in this exercise and analysis has many other benefits. We all know two heads are better than one unless both heads are enmeshed and think and act alike due to the emotional process of being anxious. Competent leaders thus bring diverse views and vast experience to the discernment table. They encourage different opinions and lively discussion, even disagreements. Holding different opinions and calculating error costs assist leaders to be less reactive and thus more self-differentiated. So often we find leaders prefer a management team that supports them without challenge. These leaders may not even have mechanisms in place for team members and employees to express their disagreements or concerns.[7] Many of the psychological traits leaders bring as well as their poor self-differentiation discourage such tension-filled discernment. Self-differentiated leaders eliminate the blind spots that error cost analysis reveals.

To Mask or Not to Mask?

As we were contemplating this book, the response of the United States to the COVID-19 pandemic was frustrated by a society polarized along political, religious, and even geographical lines. Questions about receiving a vaccine or wearing a mask awakened immediate and strong responses. Persons on each side were entrenched in their views, regardless of the scientific or other reasons offered to change minds. Even the reality of possible death was not enough to change people's minds, although some did so when they were imminently facing death. *Imagine you are a leader who needs to address this situation. What would you do?*

One can apply the cost of being wrong explored above to the contentious issue of wearing masks, an exercise that will avoid the social, political, scientific, and even religious arguments most often used. Remember, there are four outcomes for any one decision made: Right, Wrong, Right, and Wrong. Thus:

Enforcing the wearing of masks:

Right 1: Implement mask wearing: Wearing masks reduces the spread of the COVID-19 virus, and thus admissions to hospitals and untimely deaths.

Wrong 1: You've asked people to wear masks and this is a mistake: Masks do not reduce the spread of the virus and cause popular unrest and unnecessary stress.

Rejecting the enforced wearing masks:

Right 2: You were right not to enforce mask wearing for
wearing them has no effect on the spread of the virus,
nor does it reduce hospital admissions or deaths.

Wrong 2: It turns out mask wearing does reduce the spread
of the virus and does reduce hospital admissions and
deaths. You were wrong to reject enforced mask-wearing.

This example was given to students in a postgraduate
seminar. The students worked in teams, typically with 4–6
students of various backgrounds, diverse undergraduate education, also different political views on the topic. They had to
come up with their own calculation of *Wrong 1* and *Wrong 2*.
The students researched references to support their calcula-
tions and arguments. Some groups were against mask-wearing and set about to show there was a very large error cost in
forcing mask-wearing that was unnecessary (*Wrong 1*). They
decided there would be riots, higher mental health issues,
and social isolation. Where the process becomes useful is that
you don't have to reject their view that this is going to happen. They have to quantify the cost of the list they generate.
What is the cost of a riot, what is the cost of social isolation?
Accept the error is true, it is wrong to ask people to wear
masks, rather than rejecting this or arguing with it, they have
to quantify it.

The same team now sets about quantifying *Wrong 2*, that
masks do reduce hospital admissions and spread, but we
rejected it. The exercise forces each team to accept that masks
do work and to quantify the benefit they are rejecting.

One group split the task between the team members and
one half would try and make the mask-wearing as costly as
they could imagine, seeking a big dollar number from lots of
riots and frustration in response to being enforced to wear
masks. The other group would estimate lives saved, hospital

congestion, and improved outcomes from wearing the mask. Even taking an extreme view of the unnecessary cost of wearing masks could not offset the cost of rejecting the mask-wearing option and having an increase in deaths.

Rather than get caught up in what was right or wrong, all the teams, despite their starting points, found wearing masks in error was far less costly than not wearing them in error. As a result of reckoning the costs, the students recommended the implementation of a mask mandate. They never engaged in the polarizing debates that permeated the culture, politics, and the media that we witness.

A leader is responsible for minimizing the risk of being wrong

What was interesting about the analysis is that it did not really matter how optimistic or pessimistic the groups were about mask-wearing. When you calculate the confidence ratio of mask wearing you find there is very little error cost in asking people to wear masks when they are not needed. Even if you allow riots to take place, the cost of these are insignificant to the cost of increased deaths from rejecting that masks might work. There was a very limited downside of implementing masking compared with rejecting its possible benefits. The results from about ten different team exercises showed that the confidence level needed to implement masks and be wrong was low, about 2–5%.

At the time of the exercise no one knew if the masks actually reduced spread or not. There was conflicting evidence, which led, predictably, to a polarized media and a confused population. The media took an either/or position. You were either for masks or an antimasker. Rather than weighing up the error cost and rationalizing which option had the least downside, in the absence of knowing if they really worked or not, we ended up with a polarized and anxious situation.

Activate Your Team

Leaders recognize and engage the emotional process not only in their institutions but also in their families of origin. Differentiated leaders are "response-able". Being mindful of the ways systems resist change is important. Practical ways to discern and know one's decisions are the best possible ones benefit differentiated leaders. This chapter explored cost reckoning to minimize the potential of making a poor decision and to take one beyond a system's emotional reactivity.

Academic institutions, despite generally being risk-averse, often let themselves be guided by their budgets. Though that is commendable in some ways, sticking to one's budget also keeps one from discerning whether the decisions made are the best possible decisions. The latter is impossible without discerning the financial cost. Nonprofits and faith communities often work on a similar basis. If they have resources, they spend them; if not, they retreat to being thrifty. Discerning error costs can be informative for all institutions.

A definite benefit of discerning error cost is engaging many members of your team or in your organization. Leaders who think they know the truth of the future or who think they can determine the right path forward are equally dangerous. Or maybe they just feel lucky and believe it will all work out well. Having an informed, involved team is an asset. Some will ask questions you have not thought of, and this will affect your institution's level of confidence in the decisions taken. Hoping is not an effective strategy.

Notes

1. Friedman, *A Failure of Nerve: Leadership in the Age of the Quick Fix*, 52.
2. Meg Whitman and Joan O.C. Hamilton, *The Power of Many: Values for Success in Business and in Life* (New York: Three Rivers Press, 2010), 46.
3. Jacques Derrida, *Positions*, trans. Allan Bass (Chicago: University of Chicago Press, 1982), 41.
4. Ibid., 42.
5. Estimating the cost of a human life exposes cultural values that can be questioned. Here we accepted the amount of $10m, for a person's life following the advice in a discussion on NPR's *Planet Money*, see: https://www.npr.org/2020/04/23/843310123/how-government-agencies-determine-the-dollar-value-of-human. Accessed August 18, 2021.
6. See: https://dealroom.net/blog/biggest-mergers-and-acquisitions. Accessed October 26, 2022.
7. Jon R. Katzenbach and Douglas K. Smith, *The Wisdom of Teams: Creating the High-Performance Organization* (Harvard Business Review Press, 2015), 57.

Chapter 7

Navigating "Bermuda Triangles": Forming Relationships for Success

Leadership is dangerous and sometimes mysterious. Southwest of the British Overseas Territory Bermuda in the North Atlantic is a portion of ocean stretching to Florida and Puerto Rico. This part of the world's oceans is famous by urban legend. Here, it is said, ships and aircraft disappear under mysterious circumstances at a high frequency. Grabbing especially the media's imagination since the 1950s, today the urban legend of "The Bermuda Triangle's" supernatural explanations are disputed and dismissed. Though reports of missing ships and aircraft in the Bermuda Triangle may not be significantly greater than in other oceans, the legend suggests danger, even death. We know storms at sea can be dangerous. So too are the storms leaders endure unleashed by relationships that have formed rigid triangles. The mystery and power of those triangles, however, can be exposed and minimized.

Self-differentiated leaders manage their personal and professional relationships differently. Some leaders become

 DOI: 10.4324/9781003463993-11

reactive in tension-filled moments and make decisions without careful discernment. Others appear numb in the face of anxiety and refuse to act. Others yet find the boundaries between their personal and professional relationships dissolve. At home they ruminate on events at work and find sleep elusive. Anxious, these leaders' relationships no longer satisfy emotional and physical needs, and performance at work declines. They do not differentiate between their thoughts and their feelings and their relationships at home and at work begin to fail. They seem unable to retain excellent staff, even ones hired at great cost. Rather, unnamed and unexplored dynamics in the system alongside poor mentoring and supervision practices fuel the turnover around them. Leaders who are not in touch with their need to be liked avoid conflict and challenging conversations for a compromised way of leading. Working under a leader who portrays automatic compliance to maintain the status quo is frustrating, to say the least. They lead in a laissez-faire way—taking action only when issues become serious or avoiding their leadership responsibilities altogether.[1] The leaders we imagine here are not transformational. Experiencing chronic anxiety, fusing boundaries, poorly maintaining long-term relationships, and working hard to avoid tension and anxiety expose themselves low on the Bowen Self-differentiation scale (see Chapter 3).

Poorly differentiated leaders are reactive. Around them one finds herding dynamics as togetherness forces resist change. They blame others—a team or a process—as the anxiety is displaced. Between "It is the CEO's fault," "It is the company's fault," or "It is your fault," a situation easily becomes catastrophized as "the worst" ever to occur or is minimized as holding no threat. When subordinates herd together, a false sense of peace sets in over progress and transformation. Disagreement and dissent are strongly discouraged, even portrayed as being disloyal or being an unhelpful community member. Anxious leaders and systems project their shortcomings onto others.

Projection is that dynamic where unconscious and unwanted parts of oneself—especially personal failings and shortcomings—are identified in others, who are now perceived to carry those traits. Should a lawsuit become a threat or reality, blame displacement already took place.

With a poorly differentiated leader or system becoming increasingly uncomfortable in the face of perceived pain or anxiety, a quick fix is sought. This fix is most often a simple, linear process when complex, second-order solutions are needed. Is a company blaming their sales staff or supply chain issues for poor financial performance, avoiding questions about the product being delivered, manufacturing processes, or even the growth of a competitor. Blaming persons with little authority to bring change comes naturally to some leaders and systems seeking a quick fix. To support the quick fix, helpers are recruited, another example of the herding instinct. Our society has become adept at providing a quick fix as one more purchase or one more pill or injection promises an idealized reality. Behind these systemic dynamics are poorly differentiated leaders who cannot develop a new vision and who are embroiled in crisis. These leaders surround themselves with poorly differentiated subordinates and a team unable to take a clear stance. When tension escalates, poorly differentiated leaders often resign, taking their leadership to another workplace.

Managing relationships is central to transformational leadership

Take a minute to think of a world leader and how they responded to a national or international crisis. Next, think of an executive who led their company or someone who supervised you during a moment of much challenge or conflict.

Evaluate these leaders and their systems by plotting them in Table 7.1.[2] Then assess your own leadership in a recent moment of tension, evaluating your performance between on a scale from 1 to 10. *What was the level of reactivity? Where and when did the herding instinct kick in and what was its strength and influence? Who was blamed? What quick-fix solution was offered to break the tension? How do you evaluate the effectiveness of the leader or leadership team?*

Table 7.1   Assessing One's Effectiveness in the Face of Anxiety against Other Leaders

Reaction of emotional process	A world leader	A supervisor or leader you experienced	Your own leadership
Reactivity			
Herding			
Blame displacement			
Quick fix mentality			
Lack or presence of effective leadership			
Total score:			
10 = Low anxiety and excellent leadership 1 = High anxiety and poorly differentiated leadership Note select behaviors and dynamics for each category			

What do you notice about leadership in moments of challenge, crisis, or conflict across various domains, including your own leadership? What practices fueled systemic reactivity and which ones contain anxiety?

Behind systemic reactions are relationships that have become strained. One of the most destructive relational patterns is triangles, for they leave a leader and a system stuck.

As we mention in the Introduction, organizations are new forms of tribes. Movies depicting warring tribes include scenes

dealing with tribes that split into factions. This is not different from gang or mobster dynamics and how they hold things
together and deal with descent and sabotage. It is hard to
hold large tribes, gangs, regions, countries, governments, and
organizations together as a cohesive group all focused and
committed to a common goal. Often the splitting factions were
dealt with quickly and effectively, banished or terminated. We
are certainly not advocating in organizations that you deal
with descent in such a brutal and inhumane way. We have
created HR departments and dispute resolution entities to deal
with this type of behavior.

Tribal and gang leaders responded in this way as they
knew it was extremely difficult to directly keep every individual engaged and committed. Creating a culture of fear,
reputation and notoriety was an effective mechanism at the
time. In Chapter 2 we mentioned that archetypal leader Moses
divided those he supervised into groups of tens, with other
leaders supervising larger groups. Today our systems have far
more sophisticated and subtle ways of ensuring compliance.
Management consultant Peter Christian Schumacher advocates
that teams should be 4–20 people and always have a designated
leader.[3] He developed a number of fundamental rules for team
size and structure after numerous studies of how gangs, tribes,
organizations and even animals and insects function. By working in smaller teams we mimic the insect world. Research by
Ofer Feinerman and his colleagues shows that ants work in
teams with leaders and coaches who can adapt their approach as
tasks become more complicated.[4] Any group or team bigger than
20 ants naturally splinters into two or more groups or teams.

Organizational leaders therefore need to understand that
these team dynamics are at play all the time. Large teams will
lead to the teams breaking up, splintering, and exposing the
team to sabotage. In an earlier chapter we discuss that loss
can drive people to resist change, this is the same symptom
we are talking about here. Someone is facing loss and therefore resists or sabotages a change.

Understanding how to organize and lead not only your team but each of the sub teams or departments is important. Team dynamics are complex and can intensify in reaction to any suspected change. How to be responsive to team dynamics is a critical skill for leaders.

Mapping and Managing Triangles

Team complexity comes from the emotional and relational processes between people and groups of people. *Leadership is about mastering these while seeking to bring change according to clearly defined goals and ethical principles.* Remaining self-differentiated when one is triangulated into relationships is a challenge every leader faces. Triangulation (see Chapter 2) is the unconscious systemic reaction to anxiety where two persons or groups—A and B—are in tension or conflict with one another and unable to resolve the tension. A and B then rope in a third entity—Person C/Group C—with whom the grievances are shared and who now lives with the tension. The most common triangle is a couple and a third entity, often a child, a lover, an in-law, or even a practice (such as gambling, drinking, or going to the gym). The third entity assures intimacy will not deepen for the couple but the status quo can be maintained. Workplace triangles are formed for many reasons, including envy, incompetence, lack of communication skills, or even to avoid responsibility and gain power.

If you supervise a direct report avoiding triangulation is impossible (see Figure 7.1). The moment you engage your direct report and they mention someone else, possibly someone they mentor, supervise, or work with, the triangle has been created.

Victims are masters at triangulating other people. They are well-skilled at pulling you into their anxiety and trying to get you to fix their problem, rather them taking responsibility for fixing it themselves. Can you refrain from overfunctioning and becoming a rescuer when your direct report (or a family member, a friend, or a co-worker) communicates they are stuck in a relationship? Rather, become a supportive coach. In our own mentoring and supervision, we often use the language of: "You describe a challenging relationship and feel stuck. I'm confident you have the skill to address the situation. Tell me of a previous time you managed a similar situation with excellence." Should the person see no way forward, discern a range of choices together, and ask the person to choose one and see how it affects the relationship in question. By choosing one action among many the person owns their path forward. Communicate clearly you will remain their supporter without becoming their rescuer. Empower those you supervise or mentor to become more self-differentiated. Raise awareness should a person reporting to you assume the roles of either a victim or when they become a bully of sorts, when they blame, criticize, or demean others. Where you find it difficult not to enter into the rescuer role, limit your engagement to a few minutes and continue the conversation a few days later. When doing so, you communicate "I will listen to you but will not take responsibility for your functioning as a leader." An anxious, self-organizing workplace triangle, reflecting discomfort with the status quo, often takes this form.

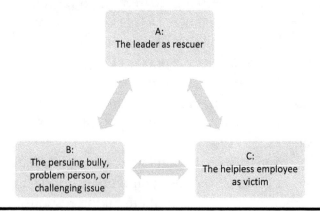

Figure 7.1   Triangular relationships.

Anxious triangles imply a process resisting change as the anxiety is passed—like a proverbial "hot potato"—from one person to another. Friedman names such triangles "perverse," for the more the rescuer or savior acts, the deeper the stuckness of the triangle.[5] Differentiated leaders can function as mentors and coaches who empower victims to function for themselves and to challenge and transform aggressive bullies to be challengers who operate with mindfulness and a clear sense of boundaries (see Figure 7.2). A healthy triangle, one that consciously engages the emotional process within a system and reflects differentiated personhood and leadership, thus looks like this.

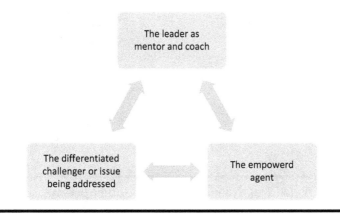

The leader as mentor and coach

The differentiated challenger or issue being addressed

The empowerd agent

Figure 7.2   Mentoring toward transformation.

Managing people is complicated. Most people underestimate just how many relationship dynamics, or the potential for triangles to be created, exist in even small teams. Relational dynamics increase in ways difficult to manage (Figures 7.3 and 7.4).

Supervising one person = one relationship dynamic.

Supervising two people, add one person and now you have six possible relationship dynamics.

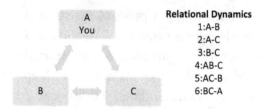

Figure 7.3   Relational dynamics with two other persons.

Add a fourth person and your relationship possibilities jump to 18 relationship dynamics.[6]

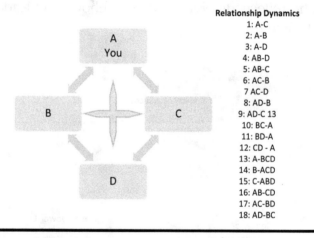

Figure 7.4   Relational dynamics with three other persons.

Facing 18 different relational patterns at any moment is a near-impossible task. And our example is but a small team of four persons! *As the number of direct reports increases, the number of relationship dynamics increases exponentially and the potential for the leader to be triangulated grows significantly.*

Leaders can anticipate the moment of being triangulated as the action is preceded by select systemic reactivity:

■ When employees are easily "hurt" and embrace a defensive, victim mentality.

- When you have been idolized as a leader and were held to unrealistic expectations. Idolization is often followed by demonization and attempts to destroy the idolized leader.
- When complaints abound with no real attempts to solve the problems.
- When an organization or team is blind to its demise.
- When reality is split as either all good or all bad, either for us or against us, when differences are not tolerated.
- When a leader or leadership team focuses on predetermined processes and rules, rather than standing back and "feeling" the situation.
- When conspiracies appear or a situation is perceived as deadly serious.
- When there are high levels of reactivity with a narrow range of responses.
- When groupthink has set in or some refuse to participate in the discernment needed.
- When criticism and conflict have become relentless attacks.

Conversely, leaders who communicate a vision, values, and goals beyond the emotional reactivity of a system are less likely to be triangulated. Effective leaders portray a vulnerability as they function for themselves, i.e., they take responsibility for their emotional well-being and can risk failure. Since systemic triangulation can be relentless, leaders who are persistent and show stamina in the face of high anxiety, resistance, sabotage, and even rejection have a greater chance of leading a system toward transformation. It is the headstrong leader who does not get triangulated, for a clear vision, alongside values, and goals determine their actions.

Engaging workplace emotional triangles is challenging. Just as personal and familial triangles, however, work triangles too can be addressed with self-differentiation. One reason why workplace triangles are challenging is they touch on many other factors. Friedman mentions the following workplace realities: "seniority, fairness, allotment of resources, space, employee slots, benefits, working conditions, productivity, hiring and firing policies, profit-sharing, snafus and goof-ups, and management practices."[7] For a leader, the workplace also indicates numerous relationships uniquely colored by the personal variables alongside the dynamics Friedman identifies.

In business management, the number of relationships challenging effective leadership is referred to as the reality of span of control.

Reckon with the Span of Control

"It has long been known empirically to students of an organization that one of the surest sources of delay and confusion is to allow any superior to be directly responsible for the control of too many subordinates," writes the Lithuanian American business theorist, Vytautas Graicunas, in his 1933 essay, *Relationship in Organization*.[8] Graicunas argues mathematically that a supervisor cannot effectively lead more than a few people. He built his theory on the work of management consultant, Lyndall Urwick, who stated, also in 1933: "No human brain should attempt to supervise directly more than five, or at the most, six other individuals whose work is interrelated."[9] Urwick drew on his experience as a military leader in World War I and as an engineer postwar to build his widely accepted theory. Using language similar to Bowen and Friedman, Graicunas states organizing one's energy is central to leadership. He sees a business leader as having no more than three direct reports, whereas leaders with less responsibility may oversee a group of six persons. "Strong personalities" with "personal ambition" are vulnerable to taking on too much, Graicunas warns.[10] Graicunas' view is backed by current research. Austrian economics professor, Christian Schumacher, for example, has found that "personal dominance" in a CEO— see Chapter 1 on a leader's narcissistic tendencies—indicates a larger span of control with detrimental consequences.[11]

The discernment around how many relationships one can effectively manage is both "the art and science" of leadership, Graicunas concluded. In conversation with Urwick, he developed a mathematical formula used in business administration to determine all possible relationship patterns:[12]

$$Total\ Relationships = n\left(2^{(n-1)} + n - 1\right) or\ n(2^n / 2 + n - 1)$$

In this formula n is the number of direct reports.

Between direct single relationships, cross-relationships, and group relationships, a leader can get lost in the number of relationships formed.[13] Should you have four direct reports, there are 44 possible relationship patterns between you and your subordinates. Accept five direct reports and the number jumps to 100 possible patterns of relationship. Supervising 10 persons and the relational possibilities grow to 5210; with 20 direct reports, you are vulnerable in the face of 10,486,140 or nearly 10.5 million different relational patterns.

It does not take a differentiated person to recognize managing such large numbers of potential relational patterns is impossible. In business administration, those who built upon Graicunas' contribution created *the span of control theory* (coined by Urwick). Span of control—how many subordinates can be effectively supervised by a single person; i.e., stay within the person's span of attention—is influenced by factors such as geographical dispersion, the skill capacity of the person supervised, the similarity and volume of tasks at hand, and the effectiveness of business processes.[14] We can add the level of self-differentiation of all involved to this list, for self-differentiated leaders will not get themselves in a position of having too many relationships to deal with. Also, supervising persons who are growing in self-differentiation has a different character compared to supervising persons poorly differentiated. Like Moses in Chapter 2, differentiated leaders empower team leaders to work with their teams, with only select direct reports.

Differentiated leaders remain mindful of relational patterns and their own reach

Intuitively, if roles are complex, the span of control is low, if roles are less complex and repetitious, the span of control can be higher. Studies have demonstrated that the span of control can directly impact performance and outcomes. If the leader has too many direct reports for the complexity of the tasks being supervised then performance deteriorates. One study examined the relationships between types of leadership, the number of staff that managers are responsible for, and patient and nurse outcomes in the Canadian Healthcare System. The study's findings, which have implications for the span of control, showed[15]:

- Units with managers who had a large number of staff reporting to them had higher levels of staff turnover.
- Having a large number of staff reporting to the managers reduced the positive effect of the positive leadership styles

on staff satisfaction and increased the negative effect of the negative leadership styles on staff satisfaction.
■ Having a large number of staff reporting to the managers also reduced the positive effect of the effective leadership styles as well as patient satisfaction.
■ No leadership style will overcome having a large number of staff reporting to the managers.
■ Guidelines need to be developed regarding the optimum number of staff reporting to nurse managers.

Table 7.2 assists leaders in determining the span of control based on the complexity of positions supervised. If the analysis suggests a small number of direct reports is optimum, yet you want to set the organization up to have more direct reports, review what is driving the lower span of control and adjust the variables that are creating complexity. Perhaps you can standardize elements of the role, or automate parts of the role to reduce complexity for the leader.

Depending on the nature of the position you are evaluating, we imagine you will land between 4 and 22 direct reports, knowing that at 12 reports, the possible relational patterns would number 11,274.

1. Plot each category keeping the direct report's roles and functions in mind.
2. Create a line graph connecting the different category assessments.
3. Estimate the average spread and draw a vertical line to indicate the position.
4. The drawn line, in turn, points to the number of direct reports for the position.

In the example of assessing the span and control of a charge nurse who had 17–18 direct reports, the dotted line shows the current structure. Mapping out, with the charge

Table 7.2 Reckoning Span of Control

Job title:											
Evaluation complete by:											
Date:											
The number of current direct reports:	Unique—almost an art form	Task management requires close supervision		Process Management—appropriate balance between supervision and process design				Self-managed—processes, procedures, and performance well understood—light supervision		Consider automation	
	1	2	3	4	5	6	7	8	9	10	
				Nature of work							
Each task is highly complex. Many different types of activities are done within the task											Each task is very simple
				Similarity of activities							
Very different—require advanced skills, knowledge, and experience											Identical

(Continued)

Table 7.2 (Continued) Reckoning Span of Control

	Unique—almost an art form	Task management requires close supervision	Process Management—appropriate balance between supervision and process design	Self-managed—processes, procedures, and performance well understood—light supervision	Consider automation	
Job title:						
Evaluation complete by:						
Date:						
The number of current direct reports:						
Tasks highly formalized—procedures and processes are in place						
Very few formal processes—make it up as you go along						Everything was documented and every task was performed to procedure
Clarity of organization						
High matrix organization with many reporting lines						Very clear and hierarchical

(Continued)

Table 7.2 (Continued)   Reckoning Span of Control

Job title:						
Evaluation complete by:						
Date:						
The number of current direct reports:						
Degree of task certainty	Unique—almost an art form	Task management requires close supervision	Process Management—appropriate balance between supervision and process design	Self-managed—processes, procedures, and performance well understood—light supervision	Consider automation	The task is done the same way every time and over time
Task requires at the time analysis and interpretation of staff and team						
Impact of quality standards is not met						
High—risk to individuals, patients, reputation, and financial						Low risk of poor quality performance—activity can be reworked indefinitely

(Continued)

Table 7.2 (Continued)   Reckoning Span of Control

	Unique—almost an art form / Task management requires close supervision	Process Management—appropriate balance between supervision and process design	Self-managed—processes, procedures, and performance well understood—light supervision	Consider automation
Job title:				
Evaluation complete by:				
Date:				
The number of current direct reports:				
Employee turnover	High			Low
Supervisor's experience and skill in leading staff	Low			High
Staff's experience and skill level in the task being performed	Low			High
Supervisor's burden of nonsupervisory duties	High—budgets, finances, meetings, initiatives, projects, training			Low—spends high percentage of time with staff or interface groups

(Continued)

Table 7.2 (Continued) Reckoning Span of Control

	Unique—almost an art form	Task management requires close supervision	Process Management—appropriate balance between supervision and process design	Self-managed—processes, procedures, and performance well understood—light supervision	Consider automation
Job title:					
Evaluation complete by:					
Date:					
The number of current direct reports:					
Degree of coordination required	High				Low
Availability of staff assistance	None—You are on your own				Many
Geographic locations	Spread over many locations and cultures—global				All in the same place

(Continued)

Table 7.2 (Continued) Reckoning Span of Control

	Unique—almost an art form	Task management requires close supervision	Process Management—appropriate balance between supervision and process design	Self-managed—processes, procedures, and performance well understood—light supervision	Consider automation
Job title:					
Evaluation complete by:					
Date:					
The number of current direct reports:					
Operations Stable—the process does not change day to day					
High unstable—every day is a new day					Very repeatable task—every day is the same
Performance of your task is highly dependent on other groups					
Highly dependent on others to complete the task					Completely independent task not tied to other groups

(Continued)

Table 7.2 (Continued)   Reckoning Span of Control

		Ability to complete whole task—plan, do, review, and act					
		Unique—almost an art form	Task management requires close supervision	Process Management—appropriate balance between supervision and process design	Self-managed—processes, procedures, and performance well understood—light supervision	Consider automation	
Job title:							
Evaluation complete by:							
Date:							
The number of current direct reports:							
	Low—many approvals and organizational hurdles						High—complete autonomy and the ability to self-measure and self-correct performance
				Level of self-differentiation			
	Low						High
Direct reports based on recommended span of control		4 6	8	10 12 14 16	18 20	22	

nurse, the complexity of their role, it was deemed that 12 reports might be more optimal (Table 7.3). Based on this, the decision was taken to adjust the reporting structure and reduce the number of direct reports for the position.

Leaders who map their relationships have a higher level of effectiveness and discern change and a lower risk of getting stuck in destructive triangles. Triangles need not be an unconscious reaction to anxiety in a system. Rather, be deliberate about the formation of your relationships. Bringing change to a people and system seeking to avoid that very change is challenging, but possible. Span and control theory complements the discussion of triangles within the emotional process of personal and professional relationships.

Triangles as an Invitation for Differentiated Leadership

"Emotional triangles are the building blocks of any relationship system. They are its molecules. They follow their universal laws, totally transcending the social science construction of reality, and they seem to be rooted like protoplasm itself," writes Friedman.[16] "[They] function predictably, irrespective of the gender, class, race, culture, background, or psychological profile of the people involved, and also irrespective of the relational context, family or business, the kind of business, or the nature or severity of the problem."[17] Since emotional triangles form when anxiety or discomfort sets in, interlock, and seek to preserve themselves and the status quo, they demand a different kind of leader, one who can handle the stress triangles induced in the most responsible person, the rescuer.

Table 7.3 Limiting the Negative Consequences of Span of Control

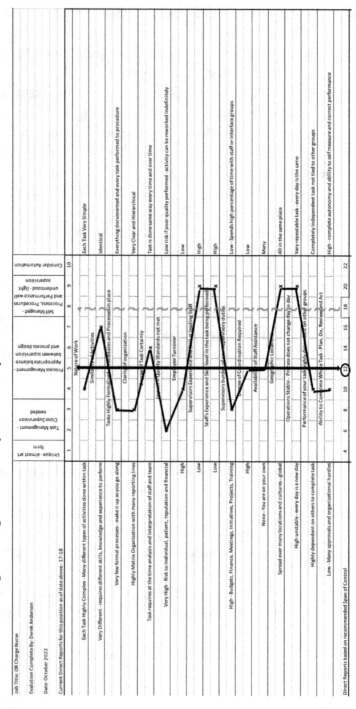

Job Title: OR Charge Nurse

Evaluation Complete By: Derek Anderson

Date: October 2022

Current Direct Reports for this position as of date above - 17-18

Direct Reports based on recommended Span of Control

The likely scenarios that will find a leader being triangulated are known, as this chapter indicates. As such, finding
oneself in triangles becomes an invitation for any leader to
step forward as a less anxious change agent. Of course, the
danger of a leader being caught in triangles and the relationship dynamics unfolding in unconscious ways are always
there. Knowing a system is anxious as the triangles seek to
sabotage change and ultimately one's leadership places a
leader in a position of proactive engagement. Mapping out
relationships is arguably the best way to do so, a task becoming impossible if the relational dynamics are numerous, as the
span of control theory indicates. The invitation at the core of
a triangle is getting out of gridlock and opening the possibility
for change, whether it is in one's personal life, or for a team
or corporation. Since one can only change a relationship of
which one is directly a part, being in a triangle can be a gift.
But only if one is differentiated enough to not regress to being
the rescuer.

Hidden deep within addressing emotional triangles is the
promise of less stress. Contemporary culture often sees stress
as a sign of overwork, possibly even burnout. Though it is not
easy to measure, much of a leader's stress comes from being
stuck in destructive triangles. Being responsible for bringing
change to a system and mentoring subordinates to become
more differentiated anticipates stress, but not as much stress
as even a few stuck triangles induce. No leader will flourish
without the ability to notice emotional triangles and the skill
to de-triangle and empower persons to function for themselves. When you have responsibility to bring change that
outweighs your sanctioned authority to bring change, leading
above your leadership position, you have been triangled by
your institution.

Notes

1. Diane Doran et al., *Impact of the Manager's Span of Control on Leadership and Performance* (Canadian Health Services Research Foundation, 2004), 2. http://www.nursingleadership.org.uk/publications/doran2_final.pdf.
2. Adapted from Friedman, *A Failure of Nerve: Leadership in the Age of the Quick Fix*, 60. Friedman discussed the first column only.
3. Schumacher first named groups of 4-20 in a course he taught, with Roger P. Maitland, at Brunel University. Quoted in: John Child, *Organization: A Guide to Problems and Practice* (New York: SAGE Publications, 1984), 36.
4. Ofer Feinerman et al., "The Physics of Cooperative Transport in Groups of Ants," *Nature Physics* 14, no. 7 (2018): 683.
5. Friedman, *A Failure of Nerve: Leadership in the Age of the Quick Fix*, 215.
6. The relationship dynamics shown are based on the mathematic formula developed by Graicunas and Urwick, discussed in the next paragraphs. See: https://theinvestorsbook.com/span-of-control-in-management.html#:~:text=The%20greater%20the%20number%20of%20management%20levels%2C%20the,one%20executive%20can%20handle%20three%20to%20eight%20subordinates. Accessed October 26, 2002. See also: Vytautas A. Graicunas, "Relationship in Organization" in *The Early Sociology of Management and Organizations: Papers on the Science of Administration*, ed. Luther Gulick, Lyndall Urwick, and Kenneth Thompson (New York: Routledge, 2003), 195.
7. Friedman, *A Failure of Nerve: Leadership in the Age of the Quick Fix*, 208.
8. Graicunas, *The Early Sociology of Management and Organizations: Papers on the Science of Administration*, 191.
9. Lyndall Urwick, "Organization as a Technical Problem" in *The Early Sociology of Management and Organizations: Papers on the Science of Administration*, eds. Luther Gulick, Lyndall Urwick, and Kenneth Thompson (New York: Routledge, 2003), 55.

10. Graicunas, in *The Early Sociology of Management and Organizations: Papers on the Science of Administration*, 192.
11. Christian Schumacher, Organizational Structure and Ceo Dominance. *Journal of Organization Design* 10, no. 1 (2021): 19.
12. See: https://theinvestorsbook.com/span-of-control-in-management.html#:~:text=The%20greater%20the%20number%20of %20management%20levels%2C%20the,one%20executive%20can %20handle%20three%20to%20eight%20subordinates. Accessed October 26, 2002. See also: Graicunas, in *The Early Sociology of Management and Organizations: Papers on the Science of Administration*, 195.
13. Ibid., 193.
14. Doran et al.
15. Ibid.
16. Friedman, *A Failure of Nerve: Leadership in the Age of the Quick Fix*, 205.
17. Ibid.

Conclusion: Showing Up as a Whole Person

Leadership is a privilege of responsibility. When things are moving in positive directions or even exceeding expectations, the satisfaction and sense of accomplishment one can experience from leading others induces a natural high. It is being at an oasis in a desert. All leaders, however, experience dry spells, times when life becomes a futile grind, moments leave us exasperated, overwhelmed, or just feeling stuck. In those moments we begin to look at new employment possibilities, for the excitement new beginnings bring is a short-term antidote against burnout. *Leadership is mastering an emotional and relational process within a system while seeking to bring change according to clearly defined goals and ethical principles. It relies on the self a leader brings to their leadership, alongside experience, cognitive-rational skills, and abilities. As such, a leader is someone who can create space for a particular community needing change and seeking to reach certain goals in the face of anxiety and resistance.* Leadership is an art, for creating space demands creativity, persistence, and out-of-the-box thinking artists know intimately.

Leadership is also risky. One can lead in such a way that one becomes lost in a sea of anxiety. Some leaders seem immune to anxiety as they gallantly lead others into deserts. We say "seem to be immune" as no one escapes the emotional process. Do not be fooled by their appearance, but notice how they need to fuel anxiety to remain in power. Where the emotional process is healthy and vibrant, persons, relationships, and communities flourish. Sound and ethical decisions are made for the greater good. Individuals in the system, as the system itself, move to higher levels of differentiation. Where the emotional process is chronically anxious, however, one can expect the opposite. Between foundering relationships and systems, individuals regress and need to hide their unethical choices. Soon the anxiety enters the physical body. Some leave, some get sick or burn out, and others yet need to go to extremes to keep the illusion of power. The stress show on their bodies and faces. Examples of leaders representing these two possible paths of leadership abound. Sometimes we think poorly differentiated leaders are the only kind of leaders societies produce. These leaders never show up as whole persons who function for themselves and who continually self-differentiate.

Leadership is the emotional and relational process of creating space for change to occur

The Essence of Leadership explored the inner world of the leader and offered discernment of different pathways to facilitate change. We looked at the unique self a leader brings, embodying traits supporting the leading others: feeling deeply and being passionate, being self-assured, preferring to create new possibilities, and having an exciting self-seeking to instill pleasure. These very traits, however, easily become one's Achilles' heel. Leading from a compromised position rarely results in the desired outcomes. We place the self in a system determined by an emotional process. One can argue there is no such person as a leader, only a leader embedded in personal and professional relationships leading others. Despite the obvious nature of this statement— a leader leads others— leaders or a leadership team ("us") easily find themselves in an antagonistic relationship with the many persons making the system ("them"). The larger the split between the "us" and the "them," the less likely a leader or leadership team will be effective. How to overcome this all too familiar chasm in institutions and corporations is a leader's responsibility. There is much possibility to be effective, for a system functioning optimally is more than the separate parts constituting the system.

You discovered specific discernment techniques to lead with optimism into the future and to overcome core systemic reactions when the system senses change is imminent. These techniques require you to work on your self and with others before you seek to lead them. The techniques are counterintuitive. When big business, relying on the analytic algorithmic capacity of artificial intelligence, pushes data, we recommend leaders hold on to data. Data can be interpreted in a million ways, even as all data consciously or unconsciously choose to exclude specific datapoints. Leading with partial snapshots of the past—looking through the rearview mirror—is not a recommended way of taking a team or institution into the future. Few things follow linear lines of progression, with curve balls and unexpected events demanding a leader's self-regulation and responsiveness.

Toward Conscious Competence

An emphasis on discernment does not imply leadership is primarily a cognitive-rational process. Rather, the definition of leadership is clear leadership demands engaging the emotional process. Having read this book, we assume your *conscious incompetence* and your *conscious competence* have grown. It was management trainer Martin M. Broadwell who in 1969, in a series of short write-ups called "Teaching for learning," wrote about teaching in a way that can be equally applicable to leading and being a leader. Broadwell writes: "A few are gifted with the ability to teach well without working at it. Others must learn the skill. For most of us, learning how to teach means studying and practicing and seeing what we did right and wrong."[1] Broadwell continues and says that there are "four levels of teaching," i.e., teaching from a certain orientation vis-à-vis the skill needed to teach effectively. We took the liberty of rewriting Broadwell's key paragraph on teachers and teaching with leadership in mind, keeping as much of his original contribution as possible:

> At the bottom of the spectrum is the "Unconscious Incompetent." Leaders in this box go on in the same old way, perhaps stuck in the emotional process of their system, unaware that they are wasting their time and perhaps the time of others. They think they are effective, but are not.
>
> Leaders stay in this box until they are jolted or have an experience that makes them aware of their failings. Perhaps they have just been fired, or someone new appears in the department that is actually competent and shows this person up. A good example of this is a leader who thinks they know how to lead. They observed other leaders and now assume they can lead, for it looks easy. They are unconscious of their incompetence.
>
> It only takes the first attempt at leading, and they suddenly realize they can't lead. In an instant they become consciously incompetent.
>
> Leaders who become consciously incompetent immediately seek help or move to a position where

they are competent. Now that they are looking for help the chances are pretty good that they will find a way to improve their leadership. They are willing to try something new; they are willing to admit that maybe they are not getting through to their team members or employees. We can work with the "Conscious Incompetent" because they want to become better. If they can discover the tools of the trade, they will start getting results, and they will know why. They become a student of leadership and become competent.

This means they now have been raised to the third level, the "Conscious Competent." These leaders are good and they know why. They know what will work and what won't for them. They have experimented, changed, measured, reviewed, and constantly looked for more and better ideas. These leaders know their capabilities and their limitations. They know much about managing self and leading others. They probably would make a good mentor. These leaders can now lead effectively, albeit they might have to think about leading. They have to stay conscious about the task at hand.

Broadwell identified a fourth level, the "Unconscious Competent." These leaders have put in enough practice and continued to develop their skills to a point where they don't have to think about the task. Ever driven down a freeway and suddenly realized you have been driving without thinking about it? This is the unconscious competent state. Good leaders, however, like good drivers, need to practice. There are no "born leaders," those that are naturally good.

Broadwell is correct in stating persons who are "Unconscious Incompetent" are unlikely to be changed by what we explored, should they even pick up this book. They will be bored by its content and describe it as "Interesting" or confide, "I do not know..." Rather, those leaders who are "Conscious Incompetent" and "Conscious Competent"—excellent leaders are a combination of these two categories—are the ones most likely to benefit from *The Essence of Leadership*. Certainly, we have been intentional about increasing your mindfulness and self-awareness, also encouraging you to adopt a "new" worldview of leadership as managing emotional processes, complemented by certain skills and techniques.

Excellent leaders know their strengths and weaknesses while discerning the emotional processes around them

Broadwell raises another component of teaching that is true also of leadership: Both are skills and, as such, need to be *practiced*. A rational appraisal of leadership without being in leadership does not appeal to us. As authors we continue to lead in our respective contexts. Like all effective leaders we know leading self and others is a practice, something one does with intention and grace. The latter is needed, as all leaders carry "Incompetence" with them. Place yourself in a position where the insights you've gained through these pages can come into play, where the techniques inform your discernment as a leader.

Growing in leadership competence is a lifelong journey and *The Essence of Leadership* seeks to inform your future. We imagine your sense of and commitment to leadership have been quickened; that your identity as a leader has been affirmed and has grown stronger through reading this book. This is not a cognitive-rational journey—about gaining more *knowledge* about being a leader or adding a few more techniques to your repertoire. Rather, this is a journey into *community and relationship*, first with yourself and then with ever-widening circles of association and affiliation: partners, the young, family, friends, colleagues, teams, and co-workers.

On Showing Up

Engaging the systems of which one is a part—both one's family system, intimate relationships, and workplace and professional systems—increases one's *authenticity*, experienced by others as presence, humility, transparency, and competence. Authentic leaders are more direct in their communication, speaking their minds freely without guarding against the reactivity the emotional process portrays in the face of change. Whereas Friedman urges us not to fall for a kind of manipulative empathy, psychiatrist D.W. Winnicott distinguishes between the false self and the true self. The false self is the self that learned early in life to conform and submit to the expectations of others. Every person has a false self. In infancy, we learn how to navigate the emotional relationships and systems that hold us. It is the self reading to assess whether it is dangerous or not. It is the self created when adults rage or retreat in silence, when nurturing and care do not arrive as anticipated. When the false self senses the potential of danger—possibly due to a raging parent or emotional neglect—the false self becomes a caretaker self, soothing an infant to prevent injury. It can quiet a crying child. Leaders use this self to read a room and to follow expected protocol. The true self, on the other hand, is creative, spontaneous, and does not care about protocol or politeness. The true self is playful and helps us *feel alive.*

The leader who stated, "I feel like a small boy," portrayed a well-developed, compliant, false self. He was stuck in the systems around him and avoided conflict by pleasing powerful stakeholders. To compensate for his insecurity, his false self co-opted his intellect, something the false self often does, and gave him memory skills. This leader became very successful based on his false self alone. As he quoted writers and poets—contemporary leaders do the same with data—he impressed all who met him for the first time. The awe, however, faded as soon one would think: Who are you when you are not quoting others? Where is the authenticity? Many leaders show up as the young child they once were. Others expect them to show up as an adult and see them regress into being a child. "In living relationships, work relationships, and friendships," Winnicott warns, "the [compliant] False Self begins to fail. In situations in which what is expected is a whole person, The False self has some[thing] essential lacking."[2] Leaders who do not show up as whole persons rarely succeed, despite their effort, charisma, and drive.

The life-long journey to be a whole person and grow in self-differentiation is a journey into *vulnerability*. It takes courage to assess one's strengths and weaknesses, to identify one's Achilles' heel, to ask for others to round you out, and to refuse to comply with the emotional demands a system places on you. Separating a leader's person and their leadership is not possible. Systems remember and repeat themselves, both in what is experienced as positive and in what one needs to question and then let go. Some critics may argue vulnerability shows up as weakness when one should be "strong," and leaders should maintain some image of perfectionism. Such critics are wrong: Perfectionism is playing a game one loses every time. Rather, seek higher levels of self-differentiation and trust it will inform your intimate relationships as well as your leadership in positive, even excellent ways. Those lacking vulnerability and transparency fuel anxiety in their systems. The emotional process shapes a leader to be stronger than any power or authority a leader's position may hold. A poorly differentiated leader will undermine the possibility locked into a position they hold. These leaders will lead from a position of *Unconscious Incompetence*, exposing their Achilles' heels as they do so. Others experience a differentiated person as a whole person.

A differentiated person can show up as a whole person

Leaders with Strong, Secure Feet

Surely you have noticed *The Essence of Leadership* does not use well-known contemporary and historic leaders in its case studies and examples. Where we do name such leaders, we do not analyze them deeply. This is no oversight. There is an ancient Hebrew story of a king called Nebuchadnezzar II. He ruled the Neo-Babylonian Empire for more than four decades in the sixth-century BCE (in modern Iraq).[3] Nebuchadnezzar II was an effective leader and built, restored, and secured cities and developed a canal system to bring water to those cities diverting the Euphrates River. The Hanging Gardens of Babylon, with trees, vines, and shrubs hanging from built terraces and pillars, were world-renowned. Powerful in war, Nebuchadnezzar II captured the Jewish people and their lands in 586 BCE. He destroyed Jerusalem the following year. Nebuchadnezzar dreamt dreams in a time when dreams communicated truths. He had one evocative dream his interpreters and diviners could not understand. The dream showed a massive statue, the head made from gold, the chest and arms from silver, the stomach and hips from copper, and the legs from iron—all prized metals of that time. This is akin to imagining a leader who had a great education from the best universities and business schools with multiple degrees, who had the right internships, and who has rich experience on top of that. In the dream, a small rock rolled toward the statue and smashed the statue's feet, which were made of iron and clay. The statue

toppled, breaking apart. In the dream, the stone that caused
the damage became a mountain unsettling Nebuchadnezzar.
Whereas the dream puzzled all, Daniel, a Jewish prophet,
interpreted the dream. He told the king his empire would
be destroyed, a reality that came to be a few years later.
There are at least three takeaways from this dream: leaders
know, at least unconsciously, that they constantly face failure;
it is difficult to sustain a system; and, leaders often have feet
of clay.

A book such as *The Essence of Leadership* addressing the
level of self-differentiation of a leader and the emotional processes we are a part of can easily expose how contemporary
leaders have clay feet and are compromised. Though many
leaders succeed if the criteria for success are merely building a
product that generates profit or leaving a legacy, we often find
their relational lives in chaos, with sexual boundary violations
and infidelity, poor parenting, and ethical abuses. Any discussion of a leader must include the emotional processes they
are a member of. In the United States, for example, leadership
is tied to an emotional process that sees rural America pitted
against urban America. Politicians generally seek to serve one
group and not the other. Likewise, African leaders are part of
emotional processes that include the legacy of colonization,
systems such as Apartheid, and high poverty and fraud levels.
That it may be many years since independence or the end of
a system such as Apartheid is not relevant since the emotional
process does not know time. The emotional process always
finds its way to repeat itself unless leaders do the hard work
to transform it.

The statue in the dream is telling. All leaders have clay feet.
The Essence of Leadership recognizes this and seeks ways to
minimize the possibility of being knocked over by a "stone,"
which is very likely to come as an emotional process resisting
change or in leaders' inability to bring needed transformation.
Leaders can strengthen themselves by surrounding themselves

with an effective team of differentiated leaders, by knowing what kind of "stone" is most likely to topple them long before a crisis arrives, and by recognizing a "stone" coming their way and moving aside so that the stone can pass by harmlessly. Self-differentiated leaders need not grow iron—inflexible— feet to withstand the stones of life. Rather, excellent leaders know when to step aside or use their hands to protect their feet. They do not despair about having feet of clay but admit their shortcomings. They do not allow stones growing into mountains.

Leadership Satisfaction

The Essence of Leadership has a specific understanding of how to achieve job satisfaction: job satisfaction is directly determined by a leader's level of self-differentiation. Leaders who are principle-oriented and goal-directed; who are inner-directed and self-regulating; who are emotionally responsive or flexible in their thinking, for example, will be more satisfied than leaders who have no personal and professional goals; who have high levels of chronic anxiety; and whose actions are mostly determined reactively by others. The path toward leadership satisfaction is clear. It demands engaging the work of self-differentiation and becoming a leader who:

- Listens, without reactivity, to the viewpoints of others.
- Discards beliefs and practices diminishing differentiation in favor of new ones.
- Communicates clearly personal goals and expectations.
- Presents a secure, less anxious self with a realistic self-image.
- Welcomes and values honest feedback and growth.
- Does not "need" others or feels overly responsible for others.

- Enjoys relationships with a sense of freedom.
- Respects and values differences.
- Cares about their role and function in the emotional process, more so than their rank in the hierarchy.
- Holds realistic expectations of others.
- Tolerates intense feelings and has well-developed emotional skills and literacy.
- Adapts under stressful situations without mirroring the stress; avoids stressful situations where there is a choice.
- Protects personal boundaries.
- Cultivates peace and nurtures a well-developed spirituality (with or without religion).

The spiritual component of self-differentiation reckons one is not a whole person without a vibrant spirituality. Here "spiritual" should not be confused with being religious or having a specific belief system. The spiritual element asks: *Why did you become a leader? What values and commitments do you bring to your leadership? Where do you experience mystery in life and leadership? When do awe and wonder touch your life? How do life and leadership surprise you?* Physician and leadership consultant Rachel Remen suggests "spending 10 minutes at the end of each day reviewing the events of the day asking yourself three different questions: 'What surprised me today? What touched my heart today? What inspired me today?'"[4] Mindful leadership deepens one's spirituality.

We trust reading this book has increased your self-differentiation, a lifelong task. Recognize your growth: *If 10 = "I have a realistic, secure self-image" and 1 = "I often doubt myself or force my way in relationships and leadership," where would you have ranked yourself before reading this book? Where do you rank yourself now? What can you do in these very days yet that will deepen your real sense of self?* Choose any of the bullet points indicating a differentiated leader and repeat this scaling exercise. Self-differentiation complements criteria often used in measuring job satisfaction, such as job complexity, role ambiguity and conflict, organizational constraints, social support, interpersonal conflict, organizational factors, and life satisfaction.[5]

Sometimes we regress in our functioning and our sense of leadership satisfaction can diminish greatly. Should that happen, recommitting to increasing your self-differentiation will restore your functioning. Before a crisis arrives, however, you can imagine yourself in various situations, draft a responsive plan, and reflect self-differentiated leadership. Psychiatrist Harriet Lerner writes "Whenever we are feeling very anxious, it can be enormously helpful to have a clear plan, a plan based not on reactivity and a reflexive need to do something (anything) but rather on reflection and a solid understanding of our problem... Working to keep anxiety down is a priority because anxiety drives reactivity, which drives polarities."[6] Leading from within with less anxiety or reactivity, with a strong sense of self that engages the emotional system, supports one's personal and professional differentiation and informs leadership satisfaction.

The Wisdom of Small Victories over Long Periods

SMART goals and STRETCH goals view time differently. SMART goals, a key *management* strategy, work within a specific time frame, usually a relatively short period. STRETCH goals, a *leadership* strategy, trend over longer periods, as achieving the goal is more important than doing so at a specific time. A parable such as the Tortoise and the Hare reminds us being slow and persistent often wins the day; the sage states "Rome was not built in one day." Still, speed remains a Siren call for leaders. Self-differentiation and transforming a system's emotional process takes time, even as a decision to embark on this exciting journey has an immediate impact.

The Essence of Leadership, in arguing leadership begins with the leader's self-differentiation, has an enduring sense of time. It anticipates small incremental changes over time, knowing each change builds upon the next and leads to differentiated leaders and systems. We identified starting points for growing as a leader: revisiting your personal (including relational) and professional goals and recommitting to them, assessing the primary emotional systems of which you are a part. In enmeshed relationships where "groupthink" has set in, get distance; where there is too much distance—you have not spoken with a parent or a sibling in months—work on getting closer; where you are in destructive triangles— whether with your partner or a child, another person, work itself, exercise, or even a substance—step out; where you have been doing the emotional, relational, and even financial work of another person, empower that person or team to do their work; and, where you find yourself in conflict, remain present and move beyond stuck positions. The small victories you will experience may not save the world—who can do that?—but they will affect *your* world and leadership. Feeling the freedom of being less burdened, less anxious, or less stuck, and sensing things are moving in a positive direction drive additional self-differentiation and leadership creativity and satisfaction.

It is both self *and* system—you *and* the emotional process, you *and* your co-workers, you *and* your institution or company—that define much of leadership. Leaders create spaces for a particular community needing change and seeking to reach certain goals in the face of anxiety and resistance. "Those who teach regularly should learn to teach better," Broadwell concludes his reflection.[7] We agree. Those who lead should learn to lead better.

A leader, we said, is someone who invests in persons, communities, and processes to deliver an ethical and needed change. You can be that leader.

Notes

1. Martin M. Broadwell, "Teaching for Learning (XVI)," *The Gospel Guardian* 20, no. 41 (1969): 2. Find the original version of the paragraph here: https://edbatista.typepad.com/files/teaching-for-learning-martin-broadwell-1969-conscious-competence-model.pdf. Accessed August 20, 2021.
2. D. W. Winnicott, "Ego Distortion in Terms of True Self and False Self," in *The Maturational Processes and the Facilitating Environment: Studies in the Theory of Emotional Development* (Madison: International Universities Press, 1994), 142–43.
3. The story is in the Hebrew Bible, in the Book of Daniel. Modern scholars do not consider Daniel to have been a historical person, with the book offering us a mythological story portraying archetypal truths about leadership and humanity.
4. Rachel Naomi Remen, "Practicing a Medicine of the Whole Person: An Opportunity for Healing," *Hematology/Oncology Clinics of North America* 22, no. 4 (2008): 772.
5. Nathan Bowling and Lucian Zelazny, "Measuring General Job Satisfaction: Which Is More Construct Valid—Global Scales or Facet-Composite Scales?," *Journal of Business and Psychology*, Vol. 37 (2022): 95.
6. Harriet Goldhor Lerner, *The Dance of Intimacy: A Woman's Guide to Courageous Acts of Change in Key Relationships*, 1st ed. (New York: Harper & Row, 1989), 43.
7. Broadwell, "Teaching for Learning (XVI)," 2.

References

Black, J. Stewart and Allen J. Morrison. *The Global Leadership Challenge*. New York: Taylor & Francis, 2014.

Bowen, Murray. *Family Therapy in Clinical Practice*. New York: J. Aronson, 1978.

Bowen, Murray and Michael E. Kerr. *Family Evaluation*. New York: W. W. Norton, 1988.

Bowling, Nathan and Lucian Zelazny. "Measuring General Job Satisfaction: Which Is More Construct Valid—Global Scales or Facet-Composite Scales?" *Journal of Business and Psychology* 37, (2021): 1–15.

Broadwell, Martin M. "Teaching for Learning (XVI)." *The Gospel Guardian* 20, no. 41 (1969): 1–3.

Brown, Kimberly P., Richard J. Iannelli, and Danielle P. Marganoff. "Use of the Personality Assessment Inventory in Fitness-for-Duty Evaluations of Physicians." *Journal of Personality Assessment* 99, no. 5 (2017): 6.

Buser, Trevor J., Terry L. Pertuit, and Daniella L. Muller. "Nonsuicidal Self-Injury, Stress, and Self-Differentiation." *Adultspan Journal* 18, no. 1 (2019): 4–16.

Child, John. *Organization: A Guide To Problems and Practice*. New York: SAGE Publications, 1984.

Derrida, Jacques. *Positions*. Translated by Allan Bass. Chicago: University of Chicago Press, 1982.

Derrida, Jacques, Pascale-Anne Brault, and Michael Naas. *The Work of Mourning*. Chicago: University of Chicago Press, 2001.

Doran, Diane, Amy Sanchez McCutcheon, Martin G. Evans, Kathleen MacMillan, Linda McGillis Hall, Dorothy Pringle, Susan Smith, and Antonio Valente. *Impact of the Manager's Span of Control on Leadership and Performance.* Canadian Health Services Research Foundation, 2004.

Fairbairn, W. and D. Ronald. "Endopsychic Structure Considered in Terms of Object-Relationships." In *Psychoanalytic Studies of the Personality*, 82–136. New York: Routledge, 1996.

Feinerman, Ofer, Itai Pinkoviezky, Aviram Gelblum, Ehud Fonio, and Nir S. Gov. "The Physics of Cooperative Transport in Groups of Ants." *Nature Physics* 14, no. 7 (2018): 683–93.

Frankl, Viktor E. *Man's Search for Meaning: An Introduction to Logotherapy.* Boston: Beacon Press, 1963.

Friedman, Edwin H. *Generation to Generation: Family Process in Church and Synagogue.* Guilford Family Therapy Series. New York: Guilford Press, 1985.

Friedman, Edwin H. *Friedman's Fables.* New York: Guilford Publications, 1990.

Friedman, Edwin H. *A Failure of Nerve: Leadership in the Age of the Quick Fix*, edited by Margaret M. Treadwell and Edward W. Beal. New York: Seabury Books, 2007.

Geertz, Clifford. *The Interpretation of Cultures: Selected Essays.* London: Hutchinson, 1975.

Glenn, Jerome C. "The Futures Wheel." *Futures Research Methodology* 3 (2009): 19.

Gottman, John M. and Robert W. Levenson. "Marital Processes Predictive of Later Dissolution: Behavior, Physiology, and Health." *Journal of Personality and Social Psychology* 63, no. 2 (1992): 221.

Graicunas, Vytautas A. "Relationship in Organization." In *The Early Sociology of Management and Organizations: Papers on the Science of Administration*, edited by Luther Gulick, Lyndall Urwick, and Kenneth Thompson, Vol. IV, 190–97. New York: Routledge, 2003.

Harmon, Larry and Raymond Pomm. "Evaluation, Treatment, and Monitoring of Disruptive Physician Behavior." *Psychiatric Annals* 34, no. 10 (2004): 6.

Heifetz, Ronald A. and Marty Linsky. *Leadership on the Line: Staying Alive Through the Dangers of Leading.* Boston: Harvard Business School Press, 2002.

Jankowski, Peter J. and Lisa M. Hooper. "Differentiation of Self: A Validation Study of the Bowen Theory Construct." *Couple and Family Psychology: Research and Practice* 1, no. 3 (2012): 226.

Katzenbach, Jon R. and Douglas K. Smith. *The Wisdom of Teams: Creating the High-Performance Organization*. Boston: Harvard Business Review Press, 2015.

Kingston, Amanda M. "Break the Silence: Physician Suicide in the Time of COVID-19." *Missouri Medicine* 117, no. 5 (2020): 426.

Kotter, John P. *Leading Change*. Cambridge: Harvard Business Review Press, 2012.

Lerner, Harriet Goldhor. *The Dance of Intimacy: A Woman's Guide to Courageous Acts of Change in Key Relationships*, 1st ed. New York: Harper & Row, 1989.

Macmurray, John. *The Self as Agent*. London: Faber & Faber, 1957.

Mitchell, Kenneth R. and Herbert Anderson. *All Our Losses, All Our Griefs: Resources for Pastoral Care*, 1st ed. Philadelphia: Westminster Press, 1983.

Prochaska, James O. and Janice M. Prochaska. *Changing to Thrive: Using the Stages of Change to Overcome the Top Threats to Your Health and Happiness*. Center City: Hazelden Publishing, 2016.

Remen, Rachel Naomi. "Practicing a Medicine of the Whole Person: An Opportunity for Healing." *Hematology/Oncology Clinics of North America* 22, no. 4 (2008): 767–73.

Rogers, Everett M. *Diffusion of Innovations*, 5th ed. New York: Free Press, 2003.

Rogers, Siobhan Sutherland. "Change Management: Your Roadmap to Training Success." *Training and Development in Australia* 40, no. 3 (2013): 4–6.

Rousseau, Denise M. and Martin M. Greller. "Human Resource Practices: Administrative Contract Makers." *Human Resource Management* 33, no. 3 (1994): 385–401.

Schumacher, Christian. "Organizational Structure and CEO Dominance." *Journal of Organization Design* 10, no. 1 (2021): 19–34.

Shanafelt, Tait D. and John H. Noseworthy. "Executive Leadership and Physician Well-being: Nine Organizational Strategies to Promote Engagement and Reduce Burnout." *Mayo Clinic Proceedings* 92, no. 1 (January 2017): 129–46.

Stacy, Jessica H. "Impaired Physicians and the MMPI-2: Comparison and Profiles by Impairment Type." PhD. Dissertation, University of San Diego, 2017.

Steinke, Peter L. *Uproar: Calm leadership in Anxious Times.* Lanham: Rowman & Littlefield, 2019.

Sturdy, Andrew and Christopher Grey. "Beneath and Beyond Organizational Change Management: Exploring Alternatives." *Organization* 10, no. 4 (2003): 651–62.

Urwick, Lyndall. "Organization as a Technical Problem." In *The Early Sociology of Management and Organizations: Papers on the Science of Administration,* edited by Luther Gulick, Lyndall Urwick, and Kenneth Thompson, Vol. IV, 51–96. New York: Routledge, 2003.

Watzlawick, Paul, John H. Weakland, and Richard Fisch. *Change: Principles of Problem Formation and Problem Resolution.* New York: Norton, 1974.

Weaver, Gabriella C., Wilella D. Burgess, Amy L. Childress, and Linda Slakey, eds. *Transforming Insitutions: 21st Century Undergraduate STEM Education.* West Lafayette: Purdue University Press, 2016.

Whitman, M. and Joan O. C. Hamilton. *The Power of Many: Values for Success in Business and in Life.* New York: Three Rivers Press, 2010.

Winnicott, D. W. "Ego Distortion in Terms of True Self and False Self." In Winnicott, D. W. *The Maturational Processes and the Facilitating Environment: Studies in the Theory of Emotional Development,* 140–52. Madison: International Universities Press, 1994.

Index

Page numbers in italic indicates *figure* and **bold** indicate table respectively

Printed in the USA
CPSIA information can be obtained
at www.ICGtesting.com
LVHW020602170924
791293LV00001B/98